THREE WORDS
FOR A
VULNERABLE MAN

JAY SORWIN

Jasid Publishing

ISBN: 978-0-578-21010-0

I would like to thank the library staff of the Orange City Library in Orange City, Iowa. Without their assistance, this short memoir would not have been possible.

Before skies and seas
Or clouds and rain,
Before flowers and bees
Or golden grain,
Before air to breathe
Or eyes to see,
Before there was earth
There was only Thee,
But thou didst know me!

Ephesians 1:4

INTRODUCTION

The story that I hope you are about to read is true. The names of characters have been changed to protect their identity, with one exception. "Maria" the receptionist is/was real in every way, but she appeared in my life when I was in Iowa. And in the process of reading, if you surmise that this story is not written by a professional writer, you would be correct. I am a retired gentleman, a senior many times over, and a Vietnam vet. Becoming an author was never an aspiring goal of mine, not until I began examining my life and asking why. Why did I have so little memory of my childhood? Why did things happen the way they did? Why this and why that?

I then concluded that maybe God wanted me to write my story to bring attention to what can befall a child when he or she enters the adult world and unwittingly is psychologically, emotionally, socially, and spiritually handicapped. When there is little or no nurturing, there is very little, then, for a child to model, and that leaves them vulnerable and gullible. One of my counselors used this two-word term to describe the attitude of my parents' idea of how to raise children, "innocent ignorance," and I find that most appropriate. This fact will be seen in the story.

Thus, if any parents see themselves in this story, please, don't be afraid of showing affection to your spouse, in front of your children, or showing affection to your children. Be interested in their interests. Praise them for something well done. Validate them. Nurture them in every way, especially spiritually.

If there are any young people who can identify with what I experienced, please do not do what I did and live with it hoping that someday some day things will change. Things won't change, but only become a habit. Talk to someone, preferably a minister or a counselor.

I hate to think how many times during my life I asked God to forgive me for being an abomination before Him. If one is a sincere Christian, that person will hate sin. I can remember years ago, when cigarettes could be purchased in a grocery aisle. I once took a pack without paying for it because I was that low on cash. I still think of that time. Being around someone who swears a lot hurts my heart. I don't want to hear it. And after every sexual encounter, whether with a prostitute, with a girlfriend, or someone in a theatre, I felt guilt. When I arrived home I would avoid a mirror because I didn't want to see my sorry self. So, as a Christian, I hate sin, and whether it be stealing, swearing, or if it is of a sexual nature, I will also hate myself. This is not a pleasant way to live a life, young people. Yet, this is how I lived almost my entire adult life

Yes, I suppose emotionally or psychologically I could make a valid excuse for my sexual activity. I think sex in a way validated me, or it was the only means of enjoyment and perhaps the only feeling of fulfilment I could realize. It filled an empty space temporarily. And who doesn't desire enjoyment and fulfilment in their life? Before I knew it or even realized it, I became a sex addict and began living a double life, and a double life becomes a habit. With little or no understanding, you plod on, day after day after day, not having the good sense even as a Christian to seek help. Please, young people, do not live this way. I have already lived it and it isn't pleasant.

1

"What a difference a day makes, twenty-four little hours," so the song goes. One day can make a huge difference in a life, but more often than not, it's a few seconds in that day that can change lives. It could be a job promotion, a nice bonus, meeting someone special, an engagement, or sadly, a terrible accident. For Adam Mohringa, none of these occurrences are what made the difference in his life one afternoon on his way home from work. How could it be described? It was like a bolt out of the blue, and the only change for him would be his residence. In an instant he knew that in a short period of time, he no longer would be a resident of Grand Rapids or the state of Michigan.

"I'll never go back to Iowa," he had always said. He loved the city. He loved all the various concerts that came to the city, the symphony, the festivals and The Celebration on The Grand that was held every year. And he liked the fact that he was only minutes away from beaches, and not very far from what the northern part of the state had to offer. As an avid but ameteur photographer, he especially appreciated the fall colors the state could show, depending on the climate that particular year. And there were so many small, quaint towns that he found during his many road tours in the fall that he thought could possibly be a nice retirement town someday.

These thoughts were meandering through his mind as he patiently watched a sports channel and then switched to the news. He was anxious, eager to see a different counselor. His appointment was set for 10:00 a.m., but it was only 9:00 a.m., and he was ready to go.

Hopefully, this counselor could give him some answers, some insights or understanding regarding his life and how he could have allowed himself to become a felon, of all things! But what a piece of paper said about him was totally different from who he really was. Or was it? He hoped it was.

How many months, how many appointments he had kept with a previous counselor who had offered no help whatsoever, not one hint of an answer to what he had done and why. The only question he would ask is, "What do you want to talk about today?" And once he asked, "Tell me about your mother and father."

Adam was free of his ankle bracelet. The past was now behind him and he decided enough was enough with this counselor. Was he really licensed? What was his degree, if any? Perhaps the fact that he said he had been a used car salesman at one time should have been an omen. Or the fact that his office was in the basement of an older building on Kalamazoo Street was a clue. But Adam chose him because the Yellow Pages indicated that he was a Christian counselor and was only minutes away. It couldn't have been more convenient.

Adam could hear the news but wasn't listening to it. He wanted to get going, but he still had an hour. He decided that he would stop at one of his favorite spots, Bonnie's Bakery, and have a cup of coffee and a fresh roll or donut. Maybe if he could be so lucky he could find a Detroit Free Press and work the crossword puzzle. Bonnie always had newspapers usually piled on one table. There was nothing more enjoyable for Adam than the morning newspaper, a fresh cup of coffee, and a roll or a nice breakfast. And now, thanks to an old girlfriend, he had another simple pleasure: crossword puzzles. In fact, he thought he might have another addiction, other than smoking. That new interest and love was the only positive thing to come out of another failed relationship, which in the end was a good thing. She ended the relationship because she decided to return to her unfaithful guy that she had been seeing for sometime, simply because he had a lot of money and property. That was important to her and Adam couldn't compete or come close to satisfying that aspect for her. And, it wasn't important to Adam, and she sensed that.

But the breakup really hurt. For a month he couldn't eat, couldn't sleep. How he had managed to continue working, he didn't know. Then one day it dawned on him: she wasn't rejecting him because of who he was, but because he didn't have enough money! Then he felt sorry for her, and the heartache and feelings of rejection lifted and he could put a smile on his face again.

It was just another failed relationship in a long line of many. If it wasn't one thing it was another, and not always Adam's fault. His latest, a broken engagement, was a good example. Thanks to her mother he learned that she had been dating other men. Apparently, after a bitter divorce she didn't want her ex to gain custody of her two daughters. If she could find a good man, or someone she could fool into marrying her, her chances of retaining custody would become more positive. Later he learned that she was not a very good mother. She would hire a babysitter and then not come home when she said she would, or stay out all night and not come home until sometime later the following morning

Then there was Didi. If he could do that relationship over, it's possible that they could still be together. Hindsight is always twenty-twenty. She was a surprise. He had met her and become more acquainted with her because she and two other women were sharing a house with his sister. He had stopped by for a visit to see his sister one evening. His sister was ironing a few items of clothing and Didi was lying on her stomach on the floor not far from Adam, who also was lying on the floor watching TV. He had been wondering what she was reading.

"What are you reading that seems either important or interesting?" he asked.

She smiled, turned her head toward him, and said, "Neither. I'm just proofreading."

Adam was not familiar with the term. "Proofreading? What is that?"

Didi explained, "I'm just reading to find if there's any spelling mistakes mostly, sometimes a wrong tense of a word."

"Oh, really?" Adam was surprised. "Shoot, I could do that too. I was always a good speller and pretty good in English and grammar.

"Well, I am calling it a night and going to bed," his sister interrupted the conversation, and "good nights" were exchanged.

Didi continued, "I've got these to go over yet," as she grabbed a handful of what were company documents. "You want to try . . . proofreading?"

Immediately Adam felt uncomfortable. He only knew Didi because she was a friend of his sister, who had left the room and gone to bed. He was alone now, lying on the floor just a few feet from Didi, who was engaging him in conversation and even asking if he would help her proofread!

"Ahh . . . yeah . . . but what if I do make a mistake? Then it comes back to you, right?"

Didi smiled again, "OK, no problem. You said you were pretty good at spelling so . . ."

Still feeling uncomfortable, Adam decided it was time to leave. "Well . . . it's getting late." He rose from the floor and grabbed his jacket from a recliner. "Have a good night. Maybe see you later."

"OK," Didi responded as she followed him to the door. "Good night."

After that night, Adam became interested in Didi and asked her out. They dated for about a year. What was so amazing to Adam was how aroused he could become with her, unlike any other woman he had previously dated. And there was nothing special about her that attracted him to her, but, there also was nothing unattractive about her. So this sudden interest was something special for Adam, and that meant love, and very soon he became completely enamored with her.

Then one day, he called her and asked what she would like to do the coming weekend.

"Anything that you would like to do, or any place that you would like to go, to eat . . . whatever . . . you decide."

After a short pause, Didi answered, "Let's just wait till next week."

Adam was not expecting this response. He was so upset, so hurt, that he didn't know what to say, so he remained quiet..

"Adam, say something."

He said nothing.

"Adam . . ."

Finally, Adam, in his disappointment, sadness, and rejection, said, "Goodbye," and hung up the phone. Another relationship had fallen by the wayside.

2

Adam crossed 28th Street and Division Avenue, the directional center point of the city. He had been at the extreme ends of both streets. He often wondered how many miles he had accumulated cruising up and down Division, how many girls he had picked up, and how much money he had spent on them. But that would change—or would it? He wouldn't be living in a big city anymore unless he wanted to explore bigger cities miles from home.

But oh! The times he'd had! But, there would be no more Serena. So beautiful, he always thought. What attracted him to her the first time he saw her was the way the light was shining on her; he could see the outline of her legs through her skirt.

"What are you doing on the street?" he asked the first time he stopped for her. "You're pretty enough to be a model."

Once inside his vehicle, she offered a weak smile and asked, "You wanna date?"

She became what would be described as a regular. Why she was streetwalking, Adam never knew. She never appeared to be on drugs, so why was she out so often?

Then there was Jodi, who he met much later and had never seen before when he picked her up one evening. For some reason they hit it off and became friends for many years.

She would call occasionally and ask, "Need a favor?"

Of course Adam always wanted a "favor."

"Sure," he would say, "Same place?"

And there were times Adam would call her.

"Hey. I could use a favor, OK?"

But there were times when Adam would just stop in to visit. There were times he would take her shopping, or they would go out to eat. Just friends, but for each of them, more often than not it was friends with benefits. He would miss seeing her. After all, how convenient to have someone like Jodie, always available. But he was always available for her too if she needed any kind of assistance.

But more than anyone else, he would miss Lacie. How much he already missed her. He often wondered if she missed him, if she still loved him. If only he could see her one last time before he left. The last time he saw her she looked sad. Something must have been said, but what? He very likely would never know. That was something he had to put behind him and move on, which is why he received the message he did that day.

He turned into Bonnie's Bakery and found the parking was minimal. "Must be busy this morning," he thought. Once inside he didn't find the crossword section and settled for whatever sections were remaining.

Bonnie noticed that Adam was searching for a certain section.

"We didn't get the usual number of papers today—new carrier," Bonnie called out.

"Oh, OK," Adam responded. "Bummer!" He scanned the sections he had and patiently drank his coffee and enjoyed a fresh eclair.

It was 9:35 a.m. when Adam left for his appointment. He decided that he'd take Twenty-Eighth Street all the way west where it turned north and ended very close to the counseling center where he had been once before. That time it was to take a psychological test. What an ordeal that had been! So many questions! So many pages of questions!

"May I take this home and—?" he had begun to ask.

"No," had been the quick response from the receptionist.

So Adam had taken a seat on a chair that seemed more suitable for a child at a ledge that covered the width of the back wall. It's height, too, seemed more suitable for a child.

He soon discovered that there were questions he didn't know how to answer. True or false? Well, that depends on what is real, what is true, or what you are feeling or experiencing. So there were several questions that he didn't answer. It was quite stressful and it seemed that every fifteen minutes he would run outside and have a cigarette.

With only a few days remaining, who should he make an attempt to see? That would be difficult because of the hours he worked, and the hours everyone else worked. He should take Ben out for a special meal. What a great friend he had been over the years, especially allowing him to share his home for only twenty-five dollars a week and letting him smoke in the bedroom he used. He never thanked him for his kindness and generosity over the years.

He would see Donny later. He had agreed to meet for coffee. Why he made that date was not a wise decision, but it was done, so he would keep it.

He had known Donny for about twenty years. He was a member and events organizer for a Christian singles group. Once a month they would go bowling and Adam decided to check the group out. After arriving at the bowling alley earlier than the time posted in their flier, Adam began checking for a ball that would fit his fingers. He began at one end and didn't find a ball that adequately fit until the last rack at the other end of the alley. When he turned to go back to where the two lanes had been reserved for the group, he saw this guy also turn, jerking his head around like a woman flipping the hair out of her eyes, and sashay away in front of Adam, completely on purpose to send a message. At the time Adam didn't know that this was Donny!

So they became acquaintances, perhaps friends. Even though Adam had been passively bi for many years, he never had any thoughts of pursuing anything with Donny until now. But Adam realized that the reason for his interest now was the fact he had just been through a broken engagement, he had to move, and now he had lost Lacie. He was vulnerable. He would be without someone. But he had made the date before he realized that he would be leaving Michigan, so a mere coffee date and to tell Donny that he would be moving back to Iowa would be a friendly thing to do and he could tell the others too. But, the selfish side of Adam was very tempted to suggest something, just for a one-time thing. Once inside the restaurant, he could see that Donny wasn't himself; he had a bad headache. So, Adam said nothing. It wouldn't have been fair to him, and for once Adam decided to do what was right.

Adam could be caring and compassionate. He believed that he had a good heart. But he also sensed that he could be distant, aloof, cold. He didn't want to be that way and it saddened him to think that many casual acquaintances would see him as a conceited snob. And that was not part of his nature at all. When you feel socially inept or uncomfortable, you keep to yourself. You don't want that aspect of yourself on display. Yet, Adam always had that feeling that something within him seemed dead, or perhaps, never nurtured.

3

Adam turned into the West Side Counseling Center five minutes early. It was a nondescript building with windows making up 75 percent of the front facade. Just inside the front door was the receptionist, who was almost lost behind an older cubicle that encircled her and seemed to be too high. When Adam walked in all he could see of the receptionist was well-coiffed, beautiful, long black hair. When she stood to greet and welcome him, he halted a bit. This was not only someone different from before, but this young lady was unlike any other he had ever seen! Never had he ever seen such sweetness envelop an entire face. Her smile, even her eyes, express sweetness, love, and kindness. It almost made him sad. Oh, how he could appreciate and love and never tire of looking at such a face every day he would be alive. And he could imagine just how cute, maybe even vulnerable, she would look the first thing in the morning when she awoke. She would be shy, hide her face under the covers, or cover her face with her hands as she snuggled up by his side and pleaded, "Don't look at me!"

"Adam. Adam?"

He finally heard a sound coming from this most lovely creature that was before him, and it was his name!

"Yes . . . yes. Sorry, I . . ."

"Are you OK?" She spoke, and her voice was even sweet!

He wasn't really. Here was someone that could change his entire world. What he wouldn't do for someone like this. He always could sense a sweet and kind nature in someone, which he deemed rare, so anyone like this young lady was special. If God knew what attracted Adam, why couldn't he meet someone like her long ago? Then he spotted her name tag. "That figures," he thought to himself, "her name is Maria!"

"Yeah . . . ah . . . I was just thinking about what I was going to talk to the counselor about . . ."

"Oh sure, I understand," she said with the sweetest smile that Adam had ever seen. "I'll let him know that you're here. Have a seat anywhere."

Adam spotted a magazine rack and to his surprise saw an issue of "The Banner," a publication of The Christian Reformed Church of America. It was his mother's favorite. But before he could take hold of it, the counselor appeared from his office.

"Adam, are you ready?"

"Yes sir!" Adam replied and headed for his office.

Standing in the doorway he offered his hand in greeting, "I'm Paul Maatz. Would you like a cup of coffee, tea, a glass of water, or nothing at all?"

Adam thought for a second or two. He had just left Bonnie's Bakery but only had one cup of coffee. "Sure, why not. Coffee would be fine."

"And how do you like it, leaded or unleaded?"

"Yeah, leaded," Adam answered. "Straight up, no sugar, no cream."

"Good. Maria, did you get that ? I'll have the same, OK?"

Adam heard Maria say, "Yes sir. Be there in a minute."

"Wow!" Adam exclaimed as he looked over the office. "This is really nice. Quite a change from where I was going, and what I experienced with . . . I can't even remember his name now. And I suppose that's the way it should be. If you can't say anything nice, don't say anything at all."

The counselor cocked his head. "Isn't that a song?"

"I think it is." The voice was Maria's. "Here's the coffee for you gentlemen." She left the small tray of coffee cups on the edge of the desk and with a smile closed the door behind her as she exited the office.

Adam took his cup of coffee as Mr. Maatz handed him a coaster. "Just spent a lot of money on this desk, so . . ."

Adam smiled. "I believe it. Very nice." He took a sip of his coffee, put it on the coaster, leaned forward, and asked Mr Maatz, "Are you aware . . . do you sense or appreciate this . . . this . . . most beautiful and sweet and gentle creature you have here, in Maria?

I mean . . . really . . . I have never in my life met anyone . . . anyone like her.

In fact . . . this is the first time I have seen a lady and all I can say is wow!"

Paul Maatz also set his coffee on a coaster. He rested his elbows on his desk, folded his hands, and brought them under his chin. "My goodness! Maria has obviously made an impression. But you are right: she is a wonderful, caring young lady. Has a great family too! But . . . we're here to talk about you. I see on my notes that you were here about a year ago to take a psychological test, and the results were sent to the court. So, is that what you want to talk about? I would like to know how things have turned out for you."

Adam shifted in his chair. "Well, yes, I was charged. There's a piece of paper that indicates I am a felon, charged with a sexual assault, which wasn't an assault at all, in my eyes . . . but . . . yeah . . . that's quite a story in itself . . . unbelievable . . . how things happened."

Mr. Maatz was not aware of the serious charge that Adam faced. "Oh my! That is serious! What did you do? Did you attack someone?"

"No, no . . ." Adam let out a long sigh. "I . . . fell in love . . . with someone I shouldn't have, and . . . yeah, it's a long story. But if we go there now, it will be out of place, historically, OK? I mean, I just want to tell you what I remember about my life . . . chronologically . . . and the things that happened."

Mr. Maatz nodded, "OK, go on."

"Anyway, I just lost my ankle bracelet a week ago and decided to lose this so-called counselor that I had been seeing for several months too. That's why I called your office. I want to know why I did what I did, or how I could find myself in such a situation. I mean, all the months I wasted seeing this other guy and nothing. I'm not sure, but it seemed like the court was waiting for his assessment of me too. But I think I posed a bigger problem that he didn't know what to do with or how to analyze it, or give an explanation that would be suitable for the court. I'm not sure if they ever received anything from him or not."

"But, I was very thankful for the ankle jewelry. I could go to work—both jobs. Could go to church. I wasn't really restricted that much at all. The only thing that I had to watch for was if my pant leg was too high and revealed my jewelry, especially in church!"

Mr Maatz laughed. "You had two jobs?"

"Yeah, for quite a while now. Ten years or more." Adam took a sip of coffee. "I work at UPS and deliver janitorial and office supplies in the city and surrounding areas."

"Oh." Mr Maatz was impressed. "UPS, huh? I hear that can be a tough place to work, but a really good reference. Great benefits, too."

"You are exactly right. One cannot be afraid to work there. If so, you won't last very long." Adam leaned to the other side of his leather chair, which he felt wanted to engulf him. "The only bad thing about UPS is the harassment, which in many instances is really stupid, but has a purpose. It is directed mostly to "old-timers" like me who are making the higher wage. If they can make us really angry and we do something stupid and get fired then they have eliminated a high-wage earner, which benefits the company. So, it can be frustrating . . . stressful. You have to keep your cool."

"OK." Mr. Maatz shifts some papers on his desk. "Let's get back to the problem at hand here and . . .hear . . . what you want to talk about. Where would you like to start, Adam?"

Adam again tried to get comfortable in his chair. "I would like to start from the very beginning, but I don't remember much about my childhood at all. And to give you an idea how extensive it was, I was the first born. Well, there was . . . I had a sister before me who died from polio before she was a year old. OK, so four years after I was born, I had a sister. Another four years, or eight years later, I had another sister, and I don't remember them being toddlers or playing with them. That puts me at eight, nine years old."

Mr. Maaz made a notation. "That is pretty significant. Go on."

"So," Adam continued, "my first memory is when I was put in my own bed, a full-sized bed, upstairs in a bigger room. This is important because I'm sure I was in a crib in my parents' bedroom, which was small. If I am envisioning their bedroom correctly, I think I can remember seeing a crib, maybe for my sisters, just past a vanity and just before an entrance or doorway to a small closet. And the space between this vanity and crib and my parents' bed was maybe two feet.

"So, here I am, the first night, lying in this big bed; the covers are up to my neck. As my eyes adjust to the moonlight shining through the two windows of my new bedroom, the furniture and other things seem to be moving. And I know that there shouldn't be anything moving. So, I call for Mom. She wants to know what is wrong. I tell her that I want a glass of water, not that things are moving in my room.

"She flips on the light switch at the bottom of the stairs and I get out of bed to get the water, which she gives me through the railings that are around the stairs for safety. Now, with the lights on I can see that there is no movement and see that there is no one there causing the movement, and I no longer am fearful. I think I repeat this one more time before I become comfortable with my new surroundings and apparently things no longer are slowly moving in my room!

"My next memory, I think, is when someone is pulling me in a little red wagon on the farm yard, and I have no memory who it is. What is really interesting is that I think—I'm not one hundred percent positive—but I think I can see the writing on the side of this wagon and it isn't Red Ryder or Red Flyer or whatever the name of the most popular wagon was at that time. And the writing was scroll-like, like fancy writing, whatever. But I find it interesting that at such a young age I have a sense that this is, apparently, an inferior wagon!

"But, when I am riding in the wagon, being pulled by someone over the farm yard, I am totally enthralled, fascinated, by the fact that in that wagon, I can feel every nuance of the earth on the ground of our yard. I believe that I even laid on my tummy and looked over the edge of that wagon and watched what that wagon would ride over next and what the sensation would be. I think that may have been the very first enjoyment of my young life."

Mr. Maatz offered an opinion. "It seems that even at a young age you possessed, certainly a sensitivity, but also in some instances a keen sense or ability to be observant. Interesting. Go on."

"Well, some time later, maybe a day or two, I'm pulling my wagon around in the yard. I'm watching it . . . go over whatever is on the ground . . . and not watching where I'm going. I walk into a speed jack and fall on one of it's levers—"

Mr. Maatz interrupted. "Excuse me, Adam, but can you remind me what a speed jack is?"

"Oh man! I'm not sure I can adequately explain that. Ahh . . . OK, there's a series of rods that connect to what are called knuckles. The knuckles are put on shafts on the speed jack and on what was an elevator. Then, also on the speed jack, there was a pulley where a belt would be put on, leading to a pulley on a tractor. The tractor would run and could be taken out of gear but you could engage the engine . . . so the pulley would spin, moving the belt to the speed jack. Oh, and all together, that would run the elevator to put corn or oats in a grain bin or corn crib."

Mr. Maatz smiled. "Now that you mention those times, I do remember seeing what was called elevators, and then too, they had some kind of contraption that was in front of the wagon where it could be lifted up. Not sure what that was called, but, yeah, I guess we go back a few years don't we?"

"Well, I do," Adam said. "Not so sure about you."

Another smile from Mr. Maatz appeared. "OK, continue. You fell. Did you get hurt?"

"I think I fell on one of the levers that would be used to engage or disengage the speed jack, and I almost lost an eye. I fell, or landed, on my left eyebrow. I go running and crying into the house, and re-member that I'm lying on the kitchen chairs. And it seems that I'm like halfway under the table because I'm not sure which way to move so the tablecloth isn't directly in the middle where I'm lying! Do I move to my right or left? Meanwhile, my mother and her sister are discussing what to do with me, and I'm not sure what they did. All I remember is being under that table!"

Again, Mr. Maatz smiled. "Out of sight out of mind!"

Adam agreed, "Exactly!"

"OK. Next?"

"Ahh . . . oh! I guess I was in the first grade, because I was in the basement of our church. And I must have been in kindergarten at a one-room schoolhouse a half mile from our farm, which all I remem-ber about that is . . . it had an indoor restroom and a stool but it didn't flush. It was a deep hole and I couldn't see the bottom of it! And the seat . . . well, as little as I was I could slip through that like nothing and then I'm down that deep hole. It scared me to sit on that, so I had my cousin hold one hand as I finished what I had to do!

"But, back to the first grade at church, and this was the beginning of our Christian school, all I remember about this grade is that my teacher would stop by my desk from time to time, and with her finger move it from one side of the back of my neck to the other. And . . . I liked that!"

"She paid attention to you," Mr. Maatz offered. "That is why you remember that. Go on."

Adam let out a short laugh. "I just remembered this." He laughed again. "I don't remember this happening at all, not one part of it. All I remember is the story being told. Apparently I was having a problem with a tooth, so my parents took me to a dentist. The first dentist they took me to couldnt't get my mouth open. I guess I refused to open my mouth! So they took me to a second dentist and he used a piece of wood to pry my mouth open! And—"

"Wait, wait!" Mr. Maatz interrupted as he sat up in his chair. "I'm trying to put two plus two together here. You had to be at that age where kids are getting their permanent teeth coming in, so you would be around five or six years old—about the same age as you were in the first grade. Now, you remember a touch from a teacher, but you have no memory whatsoever of something that apparently was unpleasant, painful . . . maybe even scary. Do you see something here?"

Adam thought. "Ahh . . . not sure . . ."

Mr. Maatz continued. "You remember things that are pleasant, like the teacher's touch, but when it comes to pain, possibly, that you don't remember. And much of your childhood you don't remember. Could it be that there was too much pain?"

Adam was very surprised. "Wow!" He shook his head and again uttered, "Wow! That is telling isn't it? But, I'm thinking . . . right now, that pain doesn't have to be physical. I mean, my heart has been hurt a lot . . . and even now, it aches for Lacie."

"You're right," Mr. Maatz added. "I get the feeling that the rejection and neglect you experienced, and not receiving the love you needed, really affected you in a negative manner."

Adam agreed and nodded. "Listen to this: I'm around the same age, fix, six, and we're at grandmother's place. I'm in the dining room probably playing with someone or something. My mother is talking with her brother, who is sitting in a chair, and both of them are directly in the entrance of the living room. I can still see them there. Anyway, out of nowhere his wife appears, who is my father's sister—we were double related—and she plops herself on his lap, throws her arms around his neck, and says, 'Oh, Eddie, I love you so much!' I see this and I'm wondering what is up with that? How strange . . . how odd."

"So had you never seen any kind of affection or love displayed between your parents?" Mr. Maatz asked incredulously.

"No, never—ever! When I was older, I remember I was in the yard—don't remember what I was doing—but out of the corner of my eye, I do a double take. Here's Dad leaning on a fence post talking to Mom! 'Wow!' I thought. 'They're talking to each other.' "

Mr. Maatz sat forward in his chair with his arms on his desk. "Let me get this straight: your aunt, your father's sister, seems to be much different than your father, or her very own brother."

"Oh, yes," Adam responded. "Totally, completely. She was out-going, friendly, funny—just a great lady. Yeah . . . the difference was like night and day Dad was one of the oldest in the family and his sister much younger. And, it was a large family: ten boys, two girls. So, his upbringing, I'm sure, was much different than those who came later."

Mr. Maatz agreed. "That may be true. I want to ask you, what was it like when everyone was in the home?"

"Yeah, I don't remember much about that. I do remember Mother maybe knitting in the dining room and Dad is at the kitchen table writing . . . copying . . . the headlines of the newspaper. He did have really decent handwriting too. I remember them listening to the ra-dio. I remember *The Lutheran Hour*. Then, when I got older, I would listen to *Gunsmoke*, *Gangbusters*, and I think I even listened to *The Shadow* a few times. Oh, and then in 1955, the Philadelphia Athletics moved to Kansas City and a radio station in Iowa would broadcast their games. I found this exciting! I listened to every game I could. I copied down their names. In newspapers, I checked the sports page to read about my new team and learn how to make up my own line-up, my own box score. Then, I made up my own teams with players. I made up or found names in magazines like Reader's Digest. I had pitchers and even gave them a record! Every day, I had a team that was playing. I wrote the teams' names on a small piece of paper as I went about my day, whether in the field or just playing in the yard. And I was the broadcaster, broadcasting these imaginary games! I was pretty good too! I probably could have been a decent baseball broadcaster in real life."

"So, I'm curious. Are you still an A's fan?" queried Mr. Maatz.

A big smile crossed Adam's face. "Absolutely! I'm sorry they moved to Oakland, but, yeah, I'm still a fan—a fan for life, it looks like."

"OK. So what's next? Any more memories from home?" Mr. Maatz asked.

"Yeah . . . and another significant one, I think. I would take lunch to my father in the field. I suppose I was around five years old. When I think about that, I can almost smell the plowed dirt and the aroma of coffee. They just seemed to compliment each other. I loved the smell—or, I guess it was more an aroma But, he never seemed to be happy to see me, There never was a happy greeting of any kind that I can remember, and no thank you, no tousling my hair and exhortations of 'be a good boy.' He would just situate the tractor so that he could sit against one of the wheels in the shade and eat his lunch."

"Even when I was older and doing work in the field, or cleaning out the calf pens in the barn, cleaning out the pig pen, the chicken house, whatever, never did he come up behind me, put his arm around my shoulder, and say, 'That was a good job you did today, son. Thanks a lot.'

Never got any kind of . . . validation, I guess one could say . . . of my worth or existence. Even milking cows, which we usually milked ten to twelve cows year-round, it would be done in silence. No conversation at all."

Mr. Maatz wrote something on his pad. "Any other memories you want to share?"

"There is another one that is significant . . . telling. I suppose I had to be maybe eight years old. My uncle, the youngest brother of my father, who also farmed, wanted me to drive his tractor as he pitched shocks onto a hay wagon at threshing time. He—"

"Here we go again . . . back in time," Mr. Maatz chimed in.

"Absolutely!" Adam continued. "So, yeah, he puts the tractor, a smaller Case, in low gear and all I have to do is make sure it goes straight down the rows of shocks—or sheaves, I guess they could be called When the thrashing is done, my uncle stops over at our farm to see me one day. Apparently someone has called me to the house. I don't remember, but I do remember that I'm in the kitchen and he, my dad, and my mother are standing there. He wants to give me something for driving the tractor. It's a dollar! What do I do? Initially, I imagine that my eyes get wide, I grab the dollar, run outside, and

19

cry! I really cry! And I'm sitting on the front steps and realize that if anyone comes outside they will see me crying, and I don't want that so I find a place where I can be alone and hide for awhile."

"Now, did your parents ask you about your uncle's giving you a dollar?" Mr. Maatz wondered.

"No, not a word."

Mr. Maatz shook his head and wrote a few more words on his pad. "Adam, how would you describe your father? Describe your father, then your mother."

"Well . . ."Adam thought a bit. "The only thing that I can tell you about my father is that he had a temper and he enjoyed band music. That's it. Oh wait! He liked to sleep in, too. I can remember Mother calling for him to get out of bed. 'The neighbors are in the field already and you're in bed!' "

"Why did he have a temper?' Mr. Maatz wanted to know.

"Well, he always beat on one cow . . . poor thing. See, I guess this was a nervous cow, or, it got beat so often that—I don't know. It's just that everytime we herded the cows into the barn for milking, this one particular cow would let loose, and it was always runny! And usually, this cow wouldn't raise her tail, and cows use that tail to swat flies! Then, in milking we had to chain or tie their legs with ropes, and the tail was right there too, plus their teats, which had to be washed, so . . . the cow posed some challenges for Dad every day, and he would use his fists . . . even a fork at times.

"Then, too, I remember I was still lying in bed one day, and my uncle—the same one as before—and my mother were in the kitchen and they were trying to calm my father down. The landlord wanted every load of grain—and I don't know if this was oats or corn—every load weighed, which meant a trip to town. He was livid! And he had an enlarged heart, so that was always a concern for them. Even though town wasn't that far away, it still took a lot of time away from harvesting, plus the extra gas the tractor took, so . . . yeah . . . not a good deal for him."

"And your mother?"

"Yeah . . . she may have been more the strong one—the leader, if that's the word. She was a very sensitive, caring, sweet lady . . . but maybe too passive? There was a time, one year, when I was in high school that I went mute, I guess . . . when I came home. I wouldn't say a word. And Mother finally asks me if I have a girl in trouble. Of course I didn't. I had no idea, or maybe even the guts to get anything . . . romantic . . . started, especially when I could barely become aroused, so that was ludicrous. And I can't tell you why I went silent at that time. I mean, I have no memory of any thoughts, of anything that may have happened."

"Probably just an accumulative effect of your parents not interacting more with you," Mr. Maatz explained. "If they don't engage in conversation with you, what is there to say, right?"

Adam nodded in agreement. "Maybe that's why when I left home after high school, I never missed home—never missed anyone, even my siblings. Always wondered about that too."

Mr. Maatz leaned in closer to Adam. "Adam, you didn't miss home because there really wasn't anything there to miss . . . was there?"

Adam let out a long sigh. "You are right. Really sad to think about . . . in more ways than one. Well . . . I guess I was thinking of myself being a product of this, but to think that my parents were . . . so . . . what?

Mr. Maatz made a notation on his pad. "I think your parents were, unfortunately, of a persuasion that any kind of affection was not suitable for youngsters to witness. I think a correct term to to describe this belief is innocent ignorance."

Adam's countenance was serious as he recalled a conversation he had heard years before. "Now that you have said this, I remember my mother talking to someone about a family in our church, a really wonderful Christian family, who apparently, the father and mother would kiss each other goodbye when leaving the house, or the farm. And by her tone, how she was telling it, well . . . it just wasn't right. Must have been odd, or something."

Mr. Maatz nodded, relaxed and asked, "Is there anything more that you want to share concerning your family?"

"This is the time too when the last member of the family came around, my brother. And he had physical problems right away but the doctors couldn't find what it was. He was not in good shape. Finally, they discovered that he had a strangulated hernia and needed surgery. They gave him a fifty-fifty chance, but he did pull through."

"And how old were you at this time," Mr. Maatz asked.

"Ahh . . . I think there's fifteen-year difference, so—"

"And your memory of him, of that time in your life, has it improved?"

"There are instances that I remember holding him, in church. I really have no memory of any interaction, of playing with him, at home. Of course, when I turned eighteen and left home after high school, that put an end to any kind of relationship. I did buy him a neat Schwinn bike for one of his birthdays . . . eleventh, twelfth, I'm not sure."

Adam rose from his chair. "This is a great chair for relaxing, but I feel like it wants to . . . hold me . . . engulf me . . . keep me down or something." Adam raised his arms, "I feel that I need to be free, man! Do you have a regular straight-backed chair anywhere?"

Mr. Maatz was surprised. He dropped his pen and rose from his seat. "I'm sorry, Adam. Yes, I think we still have a few chairs from before in the closet." He noticed that Adam had a pack of Camel cigarettes in his pocket. "Tell you what, how would you like to go outside and have a smoke while I find a chair? And maybe I'll join you in a few seconds."

Adam beamed a smile. "OK, that sounds good to me."

Not long after, Mr.Maatz appeared. "What are you looking for back there?"

Adam turned to face him. "I was just wondering if you had room back here where you could put a small table maybe, and a couple of chairs, and have your sessions outside . . . you know, make it more casual rather than so . . . strict, or professional. Plus, if it's a nice day, why not sit outside?"

Mr. Maatz approached where Adam had been standing. "You know, my friend, that is an excellent idea! Now why haven't I thought of that? There's not a lot of room back here, but if I would put in a door, an awning for shade from the sun, maybe a few plants or flowers . . . I think with a small table and two chairs—"

Adam explained his idea, "Well, I remember reading something, or maybe seeing something on TV, about a counselor or psychologist who had almost like an oasis, a garden spot, so to speak. A place where you could walk around, or sit by a stream and listen to rippling water . . . you know? Imagine how relaxing that would be. Plus, I'm sure that it would be more productive too. But what I saw is the extreme. That would be the epitome of a plush counseling center. But just being outside, anywhere where you can get some fresh air, or a bit of a breeze in your face, and feel more free than being pent up in a room for an hour, or however long a session may take."

Mr. Maatz quizzically looked at Adam. "Are you sure that you are not some kind of business advisor, huh? You have some great ideas— great ideas, Adam. Thank you! I have some thinking to do, planning maybe. Meanwhile, can we go in and continue? When do we get to Michigan in your story?"

Entering the building, Adam again saw Maria, the receptionist. He wondered, if he had a choice, would he choose Maria or Lacie? He thinks it would be Maria. But, Lacie? It shouldn't be a difficult choice. It's just that there was something special with Maria. It seemed or felt so right even though . . . it wasn't. He felt so comfortable with her and couldn't wait to see her . . . couldn't wait to love her. Walking by her area, he glanced at Mr. Maatz and shook his head.

"Thoughts?" Mr. Maatz asked as he held the door open to his office.

Adam entered and responded, "Yeah! Many, but we'll just leave it at that. They're inconsequential, anyway."

"OK. So where do we go from here?" Mr. Maatz shuffled some

papers on his desk and reached for the small notepad that he had written on. "Try this chair."

"Well, now we get to the more interesting aspects of my life, you could say . . . where things begin to . . . I guess the word would be to manifest themselves." Adam sat in a chair that one could possibly find in someone's living room There was nothing fancy or plush about it, but it had a straight back with a cushion. It was just a comfortable chair. "Thanks, this is comfy."

"Good," Mr. Maatz was sitting upright, tight against his desk. "Let me hear about those manifestations."

Adam began, " It started in grade school . . . eighth grade. I started exposing myself. It was very subtle, nothing blatant. And, maybe it was so subtle that very few even noticed. But, in any event, nothing was ever said, as far as I know anyway, so—"

"So you only exposed yourself in school?" Mr. Maatz asked.

"No . . . I also exposed myself to a couple of relatives and . . . I think I'll just leave it at that. Nothing bad ever happened. I mean nothing, period, which is a surprise when I think about it. It surely could have. The opportunities were many, but I think it's entirely possible that God prevented things from happening, even when I tried once to initiate something and

in the end—" Adam looked down to the floor. He looked up and continued. "In the end I held my door to my bedroom closed so she couldn't come in, even though that is what I wanted to happen. I was hoping that she would come to my room. I had stripped, too, and was waiting for her, waiting to see if she would come upstairs She did, and then I held the door to my room shut so she couldn't come in—and she tried so hard to push that door open to get in. It took a full effort from me to keep it shut. So . . . yeah, I always felt sorry for her, and really don't understand why I acted as I did in that situation. Makes no sense, unless, as I suggested, God acted on my—or our—behalf, and . . . prevented something sinister . . . sinful from happening.

Adam looked down again. "So . . . ah . . . that's it. No more. It's embarrassing. Besides, my desire to expose myself left and I have never had any problems with it since."

Mr. Maatz agreed. "I don't need any more info on that subject. Are we getting close to Michigan?"

"We are," Adam answered. "There is a bit of a detour first."

4

Adam graduated from high school in 1959, but not with honors. He does have a diploma, however. He, a close friend Walt, his brother, and one more fellow student, left for Colorado Springs shortly after graduating. Supposedly, they would be able to get construction jobs because Walt's father was a construction foreman. Those jobs were not available. All four did find employment at a TB sanitarium. Walt and Adam became tray boys, and the other two were put on maintenance. They worked there for three months.

Walt had been accepted at a college in Grand Rapids, Michigan, Adam's minister at the time had secured a position for him at a Christian care facility. They left together in Adam's 1955 Chevy, which wasn't a sharp car. It was only a Belaire to begin with, and a four-door to boot. But it was fast on take off! Adam never lost a drag race with it.

"So where was the detour?" Mr Maatz asked.

Adam was now sitting on the side of the desk, rather than in front. "This feels more friendly, less professional . . . stiff . . . whatever. OK?"

"Absolutely," was the answer. "You're the boss!"

"OK. Thanks." And Adam began. "The four of us spent a few months in Colorado, working. Walt and I had other commitments waiting in Michigan. There were, or was, one snag on our trip from Colorado to Iowa. We were just south of Sioux City when I ran the rods out of the engine of my car, so we had to be towed."

Mr. Maatz had a puzzled look. "How did that happen? I mean, how did you let that happen? You didn't check your oil?"

Adam looked away, shaking his head. "No, I didn't. See, I was never told to check my oil. Dad never said anything to me about that so . . . yeah . . . what does that tell you?"

Mr. Maatz frowned and shook his head too. "That is . . . I'm sorry . . . really inexcusable. He told you how to do things on the farm, right? Showed you how to drive a tractor, work in the field, drive a car? I mean, living on a farm requires a lot of hard work."

Adam shrugged his shoulders. "I'm sure he showed me how to do some things, especially with driving a tractor, a car, milking, doing chores and stuff, but, again, I have no memory of that.

"Anyway, so once we get a new engine, or rebuilt engine, we finally leave for Michigan. We're not even out of the state and we have a close call. But I can't tell you what happened. I know this incident happened because I remember that Walt was so shaken that he wanted us to pull over to recover from the scare of it. Apparently it was a very close call, but I don't remember that. When I think about this, what comes to mind, faintly, is a milk truck or tanker, that turned in front of us, and then there was a bridge, maybe, plus a curve? I really don't know. I think that maybe the situation was such that God took over and got us through it and that's why I don't remember. I mean something like that, especially when I'm the one driving—that should stick in my mind, but . . .

"But we do make it to Grand Rapids, and just an aside here, for some reason, I get entirely turned around in my directions. North and south are east and west, and east and west are north and south. And it never changes, and eventually, I lose all sense of direction."

Adam leaned on the side of the desk. "I was thinking about this incident the other day, and I'm not sure chronologically when this happened. But Walt, another classmate from Iowa, and I are living in this house not far from the campus of Walt's college. The upstairs has a door to the roof that is over the front porch. We open the door one night, and throw balloons filled with water at passing cars—especially convertibles with the top down! We make a good splash on someone driving a Corvette and, of course, the driver immediately pulls over, stops, and backs up.

"We quickly close the door and apparently one of us wisely suggests that we turn off all lights, get in bed, and be quiet. My bed is upstairs, in back of the house, which has stairs, or steps, outside. My bedroom is next to that outside wall and I can hear the police coming up those steps and knocking on the door! But we all remain quiet! For how long we continued the charade, I don't know.

"Finally, on another evening, there was some kind of party—if it could be called that. I don't recall that there were that many people there. I do remember a single girl, a classmate, or perhaps more accurately, a busmate of ours. She was a special friend for me. I really liked her. Maybe she was more like a sister to me. I never had any desire to date her, yet I really liked her, so that was unique for me. But, she would already be on the bus when it stopped to pick up Walt and I from the bus stop in town.

"There was nothing unusual, nothing of significance or importance that day. I do recall listening to a religious broadcast and considering making a donation Don't remember the message and I don't think I made a contribution . But later that evening, and I don't know if I had a drink, but for some reason, I'm looking for my sister/friend and I'm in tears. I find her in another room, making out with Walt and my fellow classmate from Iowa. I fall to my knees while my classmate, totally shocked by my intrusion and the tears running down my cheeks, gets up and—I'm not sure where he goes or what he does.

"But, so I fall on my knees beside her, crying, and say, 'I just want to be so good.' I then get up by myself, leave the room, go outside to my car, open the door to the back seat, lie down on the seat, and just cry—for a long time! It could be classified, I suppose, as a minor nervous breakdown if a doctor were to be called.

"And I was in my car all night. Eventually, I fall asleep. I wake up the following morning and it's daylight, and initially I'm surprised that no one has apparently come looking for me. I leave my car, go inside the house, and no one says one word or asks me anything about the previous night! It's like nothing ever happened.

"So, I only mention this because I always found it interesting that my friends seemingly ignored me, didn't show any concern for me, and especially the fact that there was nothing interesting or significant that came of it, that ensued,even spiritually. I mean, this was out of the blue. There were no indications of anything . . . no precursors . . . if I can use that word."

Mr. Maatz leaned back in his chair. "That is interesting, isn't it, and in more ways than one. So no one said anything about checking you out in the car?"

"No. I have not asked Walt about it but our classmate doesn't remember the incident. And my sister/friend . . ." Adam had to think. "I'm not sure if I ever saw her again after that. She, at some point, moved to the east coast. But, as I said, I'm not sure when this happened. Was it before I started my year at the care facility or after? And it makes no difference. I just didn't want to forget it."

Mr. Maatz interjected. "I'm sorry. You were at this facility for only a year?"

Adam let out a sigh. "Yes! Ahh . . . well, now we get to the . . . I'm not sure what word or words describe what comes next. I guess we get to the point that has defined my life thus far, and things that I'm embarrassed about, confused about. And, again, what is interesting, some of what happened, was out of the blue. Not at all what I was looking for . . . or hoping for . . . or had any interest in."

"Is this where we meet Lacie?" Mr. Maatz asked.

"No, not yet." Adam smilesd. "The best is yet to come!" Adam thought again. "Well, on second thought, don't take that the wrong way."

Mr. Maatz shared a smile. "I must admit that I'm getting eager to hear about this young lady. But, first things first, I guess. Please, go on."

"My first job at this care facility is at a building that houses young people, from children to young adults. Basically, I'm like a babysitter. I see that they take their medications if prescribed, serve their meals, feed those who are unable to feed themselves, keep them clean and neat, help some to brush their teeth, and so on. And when things settle down, I do dusting, mopping—just general cleaning.

"So, one day, maybe within the first week, or two, I'm walking down this hallway. I don't remember where I was going or what I was going to do. From the other end of the hallway, I see one of the young resident adults walking toward me. I think nothing of it; I pay him no attention. We meet, and he reaches his hand out and touches me . . . there. Immediately, to my utter shock," Adam looked down and shook his head. "To my utter shock, I am immediately aroused, and I mean it is immediate. I mean, like snap your finger and I'm at attention, you know? How is this even possible? This has never happened before with anyone, not even with a girl. And this happens with a guy? I like girls, for Pete's sake! I'm attracted to girls, not guys. And you know, experiencing something like this had never happened before, and has never happened since. And that, once again . . . I find really interesting. I mean, how is something like this even physically possible?

"Also interesting," Adam continued, "is that where this incident took place, there just happened to be a small restroom. By the time I turn around in my reaction to look at this guy, he already has the door open and with a nod of his head beckons me in. Because this is entirely new to me, and naturally exciting, I follow him inside. And, I experience my first homosexual act of receiving pleasure."

Adam leaned forward, placing both his hands on the desk in front of him. "This incident happened right out of the blue. I often wonder why. It's almost like an act of God—or an act of Satan! I mean, really! How am I to understand why this happened to me? How am I to process this?

"Now, I didn't even know this existed. In fact, just prior to this occurrence, I was introduced to shooting pool for the first time. There were three of us, and at one point they were talking about an employee who was 'queer,' and I thought they meant he was odd. That's how green this Iowa farm boy was, but, unfortunately, that was about to change—and not for the better."

Mr. Maatz wanted to know, "And why is that?"

"Well," Adam cleared his throat and shifted his weight from one side of his chair to the other. "Being in a big city for the first time, I find all these fairly nice-looking girls standing on street corners. I remember one of the first girls I stopped for. She was a beautiful black girl and the way the light was shining on her at that particular time of day, I could see her legs through her skirt. I had to stop!

"She got in my car and I say to her, 'What are you doing on the street? You're pretty enough to be a model or something.' She offered a weak smile and said, 'Wanna date?' Over the years, I have become, I suppose, somewhat of a regular customer for her. If she isn't available, there are numerous others . . . and other venues.

"So, other than all the prostitutes, I also discover adult book stores, some with booths with unlocked doors, so a visitor can join you, maybe even a couple. Yes, I had that experience. Then, too, there were adult theatres. One that I found by accident was predominantly attended by men, which I frequented often. Occasionally, a couple would be in attendance. And finally, there were all the massage parlors. I visited most of them. I enjoyed many of the young Asian girls. Many I think were Korean and many really sweet.

"In other words," Adam said, sighing, "at the young age of nineteen I became a promiscuous bisexual guy, and Lord knows how much money I have spent on sex over the years. And even if I'm dating someone, it doesn't deter me. Am I proud of it? Not in the least. I often wonder how many times I have asked God to forgive my abominations. You get to a point where you avoid mirrors because you don't want to look at yourself. You find yourself that disgusting!" But, it seems like things become habitual . . . your life becomes a habit, I don't know."

"You're not far from the truth there, young man," Mr. Maatz added. "So I believe you said something earlier that you were at this facility for only a year?"

"Yes," Adam began to explain. "I was on the night shift, as were three others. We would have water fights, play cards, whatever, and one night everyone, it seemed, except me—in fact I didn't even realize it at the time—were on the roof of the building! Well, that got out and all of us were put on probation, I think for three months. This was in late summer.

"Come October thirty-first, Halloween, I'm with a group who want to go out and throw eggs and tomatoes. That sounds like fun to me , but I suggest that we should not go downtown. Well, guess what? Yeah . . . we end up downtown, and the inevitable happens. We get stopped by the police and end up in the police station, where we're placed in a huge cage. Eventually they let us go and the following morning we all take our turn in the administrator's office. Because I was the only one on probation, I was asked to resign my position."

"And how did that make you feel?" Mr. Maatz asked.

"Well, not so good," Adam replied. "I immediately think how disappointed my mother will be. I had just completed a milestone in my training and she was so proud of me. As for the job . . . well, it was just a job at the time."

"So what did you do? Where did you go"? Mr. Maatz queried Adam.

"A good friend from grade school, and his family, had moved to Grand Rapids the previous year, and gladly let me live with them. My friend got me a job delivering auto parts. That lasted until my father had heart problems and I went back to Iowa to help out on the farm. And not long after that I find my orders from the military in the mailbox and I am drafted into the army. Because I was a male nurse at this care center, I was sent to medic school in San Antonio. After spending three months in that great city, I was sent to serve my remaining time at Fort Benning, Georgia. It was a really easy time, until the order came, with only two months to go, that all of us would be going to Vietnam."

"That had to be some kind of experience," Mr. Maatz said.

Adam nodded. "Oh, it was. We went through the Panama Canal, stopped at Long Beach in California, but the neatest thing . . . what I enjoyed the most was just being on that ship. I would go as far as allowed on the deck because it was so peaceful, so tranquil. It was a spiritual thing for me. I never felt so at peace. I loved it!"

"So, by the time you get to whatever destination it is in Vietnam, how much time do you have left?" questioned Mr. Maatz. "Or do they extend your time?"

Adam nodded again and smiled. "Boy, we were wondering the same thing, initially. But, yeah, when the time—when our two years was up—we began separation procedures and were sent home. And I am so glad I left when I did, because a day after I left our unit apparently got hit. I only learned this because there were several who had separation dates immediately after my date. And yet, I never did learn how serious an attack it was. But, I arrived home a few weeks before Christmas. So, even though I was there for a short time, I saw enough to be glad I was on my way back to America."

Mr. Maatz rose from his chair and offered his hand to Adam. "Thank you for your service, Adam."

Adam was surprised by this thoughtful gesture and accepted the hand in front of him. After a second or two of hesitation, he rose. "Oh, thank you. I appreciate your . . . appreciation of our military men and women, but, I was . . . how can I say this . . . I was like a serviceman in name only. As a medic I am so thankful no one had to rely on me to give emergency care, because I had no confidence in my abilities whatsoever. In fact, I will say this: when I think of my time in the army, It was only by God's grace that I made it through, really."

A frown appeared as Mr. Maatz added, "'I'm sorry that these are your thoughts. Did you go through your entire two years of service feeling so inadequate?"

"Yeah, pretty much. But,that was . . . like . . . every day—army or no army." Adam raised his arms. "I mean, that's my life, you know?"

Mr. Maatz scanned his notes. "I am reminded from my notes here that I can understand why you feel . . . as you do . . . or think of your-self as you do, even though you seem to have good intelligence, and have been gainfully employed for a number of years. I see a unique and interesting individual who should, I think, give himself a little credit, but maybe, hopefully, that is to come in the years ahead. OK. So, where do we go from here?"

Adam sighed, "Well, I spend some weeks at home. I am hired by the post office and one Saturday am the only one to deliver some mail. I'm not sure if the mail was missorted at some point, or if it was special delivery, but it wasn't a lot. The problem was that I had no idea where to start, how to sort it. Eventually, I delivered all of it, but it took me awhile crisscrossing the town . . . who knows how many times? So, even though I had been hired by the USPS, I wasn't impressed and I think mentally I was not prepared to appreciate the job, and then too, I didn't want to live with my parents. So, I went to the city."

Mr. Maatz leaned forward, resting his arms on his desk. "And how did that go for you?"

Adam thought for a bit. "I think I had two jobs that were not successful. I was let go of one because I got animal serums mixed up. I worked for a feed and vet supplies company and when the boss delivers needed vaccines to a customer that are not the kind or type ordered—well, that upsets the the boss and the customer. And these mistakes continued,for some reason that I can't explain.

"After that, I run into a buddy from high school who worked for Canteen Service filling candy and cigarette machines They needed another delivery driver, so I applied and was offered the job. They put me on a route that became the best route of all for money taken in. I was then promoted to a food route servicing sandwich, soup, and beverage machines.

"This business also had a bowling team, which I joined. At this bowling alley I meet a blond who delivers food and drink to the bowlers. She's a blond with long legs, nice looks, and a very nice walk! Eventually, we date, and for some reason that I will never realize, I am totally irresponsible, and after a few months, she becomes pregnant."

"Uh oh," Mr Maatz chimed in.

"Yeah, right," Adam agreed and shook his head. "What do you do in the sixties if you get a girl pregnant? You have to get married."

"But—"

Adam interrupted, "But, I don't love this girl. There was one night when I had all my bags packed and was ready to leave the state. But, where do I go? Could I leave my parents in the dark, not knowing what happened to me, or where I went? And how long could I stay hidden? So, I decided on marriage, even though I knew . . ." Adam looked to the floor and shook his head.

"Did you have a church wedding?" Mr.Maatz asked.

"We did," Adam responded. "Can you imagine repeating wedding vows that you know aren't true and that you have no idea if you are, or will ever be, capable of honoring those vows?

Then imagine, too, at the very end, both of you are kneeling on the altar and the minister is praying over both of you, and inside you know: this entire ceremony is a farce. Inside, I'm hoping that one day God will forgive me. So, that's how I got married."

Now Mr. Maatz was shaking his head. "Wow! That is really a sad story. I am so sorry.

And I'm sorry to hear a story like that." He rose and ambled to a window. "So, and I'm afraid to ask, how did things turn out? How long did the marriage last?"

"Not long," Adam sighed. "We divorced the following year. I moved out within a few months. I remember when I left—and this haunts me a bit—as I was leaving our upstairs apartment, my wife was clinging to my arm, begging me not to leave her. But I continued, and as I got to the stairs, her grip on my arm slipped and she fell to the floor. I could hear her crying all the way down the stairs. When I think of that now, I wonder how I could be so . . . cold. But at the time I was just so . . ." Adam could only shake his head. "I was just screwed up."

Mr. Maatz also let out a sigh. "Let's move on, can we? I'm sorry, Adam, but that marriage story just hit me today, for some reason, and I've heard my share but . . . so where do we go from here?"

"It's near the end of September and I leave for Michigan again. In fact, if I remember correctly, I think it was the Labor Day weekend. Anyway, it wasn't very long at all before I found a job at a factory making car seats. I put wires in the seat frame using a special pair of pliers . . . for eight hours. And soon, I realize that gloves are a must to prevent blisters. I also quickly learn to be ambidextrous! Some months later, I get a call that Dad had died."

Mr. Maatz was curious. "So how did that make you feel?"

Adam sighed. "You know . . . I felt nothing . . . no sorrow at all. Neither did my brother. My sisters, on the other hand, were basket cases. After a few days, we all head back to Michigan, and continue with our lives."

"OK," Mr. Maatz chimed in. "Where or what is next? When do we come to that incident that . . . ah . . . enabled you to wear that jewelry piece around your ankle, hmm?"

Adam laughed. "Yeah! Well, I appreciate your attempt to make light of a serious situation—or what was a serious situation—but, yeah, it was . . . stressful, scary . . . especially how it all came about, how it all happened. I mean, there were a lot of guys going to prison for what I was charged with. I had thoughts of going to trial because I did not do what I was charged with."

Mr. Maatz raised his hands. "Whoa! Wait a minute! Why then—"

Adam interrupted, "Yeah, I know. Just be patient and we'll get there. It is a bit complicated. I don't want to get ahead of myself, OK?"

Mr. Maatz relaxed, sits back in his chair. "OK."

5

Adam sat back in his chair, looked toward the ceiling, and sighed, "OK. Jodie, my friend . . . and part-time prostitute—let me just refer to her as my friend from now on—has moved to this large apartment complex. She has met this woman named Kate who supposedly has a camera like mine. She also has four kids, which is not a problem. The fact that she has a camera is more interesting to me than the kids. I always thought it would be great to meet a lady who had the same interest as I did in taking pictures.

"So, Jodie makes a date for all of us to meet. We're all standing in a circle in the living room as Jodie introduces me and almost immediately, I get a feeling or a sense not to get involved. But, it isn't a strong sense and it really doesn't get my attention, and I'm wondering why I should feel this anyway. I mean, Kate seemed to be nice enough, very pleasant. Her kids seemed nice, so, I dismissed it. It was just me being weird for some reason, so I forget it. So, I tell Kate that it was nice meeting her and the kids. I get her phone number and plan on making a date within the week."

Mr. Maatz stopped Adam's narrative. "What about the kids?"

"Oh, right." Adam thought for a second. "Let's see . . . Kendra was twelve, I think. Then Lacie was eight, Sam was six, and Noelle was four. And, if you are wondering, no, at the time I didn't give any of the kids a second look. Not at all."

"OK, good." Mr. Maatz made a notation. "Continue."

"So, the first time I stop to see Kate, I'm no more than a few steps into the apartment and here comes Lacie, running up to me and jumping up in my arms. I'm not expecting this at all. 'My goodness!' I exclaimed. Her arms were around my neck and her legs were around my waist. I put my arms around her to hold her there and after a short while she relaxed and I slowly let her down to the floor.

"Now this happens every time I stop in to see Kate. Plus, wherever I sit, Lacie is beside me. At first, when I would get off the couch to use the restroom, she would follow me. The first time, I turned to close the door, and there's Lacie! 'Lacie,' I say, 'I have to use the restroom.' After awhile, when she sees me walking in that direction, she knows that she doesn't have to follow. But before that she would get off the couch and start following me, and then, seeing that I was going toward the restroom, stop and return to the couch. I mean, she was like a puppy dog!"

Mr. Maatz made some notations and asked, "How did that make you feel?"

"Well . . ." Adam sighed. "I loved the attention. Thinking about it later, what Lacie was doing was so innocent, sweet, loving. And, I had never received so much attention.

I loved it. It was like a father coming home and his little girl was happy to see him. It was—"

Mr. Maatz broke in. "And now things get serious—too serious, right?"

Adam agreed. "Exactly. Eventually, I'm more interested in seeing Lacie than her mother . . . and . . . I'm developing strong feelings for Lacie."

"And then it happens—"

Before Mr. Maatz could finish, Adam went on. "Yeah, and how! It's almost unbelievable how things went . . ." Adam shook his head. "I have often wondered if the judge even believed what I wrote, how I described what happened."

Mr. Maatz was eager to know. "So tell me! Let's hear it!"

"Well," Adam begins, I'm babysitting one evening, sitting on the couch with Lacie, of course, watching TV. After some time, I get up to go to the kitchen and make some coffee. I return to the couch and there's Lacie, lying on the couch, her arms raised as high as she can reach, and she says, 'Come lay by me.' "

"Oh no! Adam . . . ?" Mr. Maatz apologized. "Sorry, go on."

"So, I ask, 'Why do you want me to lay by you?' 'Because I want you to,' she answers. Her arms are still reaching for me, stretching out further, it seems, than before. I know this is not a good situation, that this is dangerous, but how can I resist . . . Lacie? So I figure I'll play along with her and I lie on my right side next to her and rest my right arm on the arm of the couch. She then raises her head toward me, cups her hands around her mouth, and whispers in my ear, 'Know a secret?' It sounded like a question, so I ask her, 'Do I know a secret?' 'Yes,' she says again. 'Know a secret?' So I ask, 'What?' She whispers in my ear, 'I love you.'

Adam let out a long sigh. "Well, those were such wonderful words to hear, and all I could so easily do is to whisper in her ear, 'I love you too.' But, incredibly that wasn't the end of it. Next, she says, 'Now kiss me.' I'm thinking, really? So I ask, 'Kiss you?' 'Yes, kiss me,' is her response."

Mr. Maatz said nothing but shook his head.

"So I'm just going to give her a kiss on her cheek, right? So I lean toward her to give her a quick kiss on her cheek, and before I know it, I'm kissing her on her lips and her arms are clasped tightly around my neck. I say clasped, because my first instinct is to rise up, which I do, twice, and I'm still kissing her! At the same time, she turns more toward me on her side, and now our bodies are close and I can feel that where I have my left hand resting, is very near where it shouldn't be! And now, with my feelings of love for her, and kissing her, I become aroused.

"I kiss this girl as lovingly and as tenderly as I can. The feeling I had in every kiss . . . ah . . . I guess I was hoping to convey my love for her in each kiss, which is a feeling I've never experienced before, never, and this is . . . a girl, for Pete's sake! So, I kiss each eye, the tip of her nose, I start a kiss on her upper lip, her lower lip. I want to kiss every inch of her. I think of using a little tongue but don't. I want to touch every inch of her,.and I do caress her where I shouldn't. This is when I forcibly break our embrace, because I know that I've gone too far. 'Lacie,' I ask. 'Why are you doing this?' Her answer wasn't because she loved me but, 'I watch TV!' I then remembered a previous date with her mother, and when we had entered the apartment I could see on TV a couple doing exactly what Lacie and I had just participated in. And that brought me back to reality a bit."

"You think?" Mr. Maatz quipped.

"It scared me too," Adam added, "because, like my attorney told me, there were a lot of these cases and innocent guys were going to prison. So, yeah, what could happen? Yet, I didn't think Lacie would say anything, but, after all the weeks that had passed, who knows?"

"Plus she's only a child, Adam," Mr. Maatz sternly exhorted, "And you WERE guilty!"

Adam nodded in agreement. "You are absolutely right."

Mr. Maatz sighed. "Continue."

Adam began. "For three, maybe four weeks, Lacie and I did have our times on the couch, but there was no more inappropriate touching. And because, as an adult male, when you are in love and you're making out, after awhile you become aroused—but if your partner doesn't become aroused, after several incidents, then . . . the fire doesn't burn so hot anymore, and you too don't become as aroused. This is what I experienced with Lacie, but I still loved her. It was also during this time that I wanted to tell her mother what had happened. But, for the life of me, I could not get one word out of my mouth. I mean, as I tried, as I thought of how to start, what word to begin with, I went completely silent. The TV would be on that we could watch, but even during commercials, there was silence. You know how very . . . uncomfortable . . . and stressful that can be? A commercial is on TV and no one says anything! It was, I think, the most frustrating period of my life."

"So eventually what did you do?" asked Mr. Maatz.

Adam raised his arms. "I just stopped going over . . . and got on with life, hoping things would settle down and nothing would come of it. I bought, or subscribed to, a singles publication and met a girl who was supposedly marriage minded, and she had two daughters. A potential family for me, I thought!

A look of concern was on the face of Mr. Maatz. "Two daughters?"

"Yes," Adam replied. "And one is the same age as Lacie and the other is only three. And," Adam smiles wryly, "she does not jump up in my arms!"

Mr. Maatz only shook his head.

"Then some months later I come home from work one day, and on the kitchen table I find a postcard from the juvenile section of the police department. They want me to come in at eight o'clock the following morning. Of course I know what this will be about."

His eyebrows raised and the furrows in his forehead were easy to see as Mr. Maatz said, "This should be interesting."

Adam nodded quickly. "It is." He looked to the floor and repeated, "It is. First of all, I discover that this has nothing to do with Lacie, apparently, because it's her sister, Kendra, who says that I put my finger inside of her—which never happened. And I wonder if someone put her up to this. I can't believe her mother goes along with this, either, or doesn't question her. I mean, I'm sorry, I have to get personal here. Her mother knows me—knows what I like to do, OK? I'm a sensual man and I enjoy pleasing a lady sensually, and her mother has experienced that pleasure. So, if I had the guts to get that far with Kendra, all I'm going to do is just use a finger? Really? That makes no sense! And it shouldn't make any sense to the detective, either. At least they should question it. And then she says to me, 'Well, the doctor said she wasn't harmed in any way.' And in my surprise I blurt out, 'She went to a doctor?' "

Adam continued the narrative. "Now, there was a time when she was really angry with me. I had seen a picture in a magazine of a girl, or a young lady, standing in a field of flowers. Kendra happened to be there and I voiced my desire to take a picture like that with her. What attracted me to this picture was that you could see the outline of her legs through the dress she was wearing, so I asked if she had any flesh-colored leotards. She didn't, and I didn't know of any fields of flowers, so nothing much was said about it. So, fast forward: I'm babysitting one night and I'm intently watching the TV show *Dallas*. I was a serious follower of this show. During an intense scene, Kendra, out of the blue, asks me, 'What should I wear under my dress for that picture?' Because I'm so into this show, and we haven't even discussed this picture for some time, I just say, 'Nothing.' Her mother and a friend come home from a girls night out, and Kendra cries out, while she jumps up from the couch and runs upstairs, 'Mom, Adam is weird. He wants to take a picture of me with nothing on under my dress.' And for the first time in my life I wish I could disappear some-where in that couch! But, to my surprise, her mother says nothing. No questions, nothing. And I, in my . . . utter stupidity, or inability to defend myself . . . whatever . . . say nothing. Didn't even occur to me! When I think of this fact it just amazes me how dumb that is. I don't understand that."

Mr. Maatz leaned forward in his chair and in a calm voice said, "I think, Adam, that you didn't defend yourself because in a way you harbored some guilt. I think that the kind of photos you wanted to take—somewhat sensual, revealing, especially legs—is why you didn't speak up. And yes, you are the type of person who will not stand up for yourself. So, eventually, what happens? How does this all come to an end?"

6

Adam hired the best attorney that was available. When Adam recount-
ed the incident with Lacie, but denied Kendra's charge, his attorney
suspected a kind of transference and requested he take a psychological test. He also set up a lie detector test for Adam. The results were
never revealed to Adam. He also took a lie detector test at the police
station, which he also never learned the results of. He thinks he did
OK because he was more relaxed with that one than the private one
his attorney set up.

No one was aware of his situation, or predicament, and he didn't
inform anyone, either, until a week before his court date. He then told
Ben and he told his sister what he had been charged with. She put
him on a prayer list. His friend Jodie had known for some time, but
not the truth concerning Lacie.

On the day before his court date, a Sunday, Adam was stressed
and told Ben that he was going for a ride, which wasn't exactly true.
Adam just wanted to be alone and randomly drives. He wasn't sure
where to go so he turned on his favorite street, Division Avenue,
and headed toward downtown. He turned on West Fulton, and after a few blocks stopped at an overpass. Because it was Sunday,
there was very little traffic and no pedestrians. It was a quiet place
where one could be alone, under an overpass, where Adam carefully treaded on rocks and found a spot to sit. His arms were resting
on his knees, his head was down, and then the tears fell. After a few
minutes, his body began to jerk with sobs. He allowed the tears and

mucus to drip wherever it wanted.

He sat there in the same position for maybe an hour. He didn't know. He finally wiped his nose and did his best to deposit the mix on a rock. He noticed a restaurant across the Grand River, and wondered if anyone dining could see that he was crying. Would they notify anyone, to check on him? What would he do then? It would be embarrassing, he thought. But to have someone who cared and would make an effort to see if he needed or wanted assistance would be appreciated. But no one came and Adam just continued to sit there. He still was sad, depressed, stressed, afraid, and felt so alone, so helpless. He finally cried out to God, "Please, help me, God, please help me!" And he cried some more.

After some time, the tears stopped and Adam felt somewhat relieved. He would have to wait for the swelling around his eyes and the redness to disappear before he could go home and be presentable for Ben. Maybe he could find a convenience store and get a cup of coffee. No one would know who he was anyway. He could use a restroom and rinse his face too.

But one thing was certain: tomorrow at this time he would more than likely know the consequences of innocently falling in love with someone very special, but legally and morally unacceptable. He knew this, but couldn't understand how something like this could happen. Sure, he wanted to love someone special, and to be loved, but with Lacie? And it all happened in innocence. Yet, he would certainly be found guilty—guilty for falling in love.

That evening, before Adam went to bed, he lay prone on the floor beside his bed in fervent prayer. He also prayed that Jodie would not forget that she was to pick him up and take him to the courthouse in the morning. Thankfully, she was on time and wished him good luck.

Adam heard the proceedings, but nothing made sense. He was given the opportunity to make a statement, which he did in a quivering voice. The judge then rendered his decision, which Adam heard but still did not understand. He did hear "six months," and then it was like blah, blah, blah. After the judge adjourned, his attorney related the decision and his sentence. It was six months house arrest, but he would be able to continue his jobs at UPS and his delivery job. He would even be able to go to church on Sunday. So, he was free to do continue his life as before, except when he is to be confined to 'house arrest,' he cannot be more than one hundred feet from the house.

After sitting for so long, Adam stretched, raising his arms and pushing his legs far out in front. "So I'm glad that aspect of my life is over. I'm happy . . . pleased with the court's decision, even though a piece of paper says that I'm a felon. I don't see myself that way at all. A piece of paper doesn't define who I really am, so, I mean, I'm not proud of, this record . . . of what I did and what happened. It's just something that happened. It's over, it's past . . . so move on, forget about it."

"Besides," Adam continued, "as I said before, God did try to warn me by giving me that sense of not getting involved and I ignored it, so, I take full responsibility for what happened."

Mr. Maatz agreed. "I think that is an acceptable attitude to take. Our time is up, Adam, and just a quick assessment from what I take away from our visit today. I offer you these words: no sexual identity. Does that make any sense?"

"Absolutely! Those three words make more sense than all the months I spent with the other guy!" Adam offered his hand to Mr. Maatz. "Thank you so much."

Mr. Maatz took Adam's hand and held it. "I almost forgot: you requested an extended session because you're returning to Iowa, so this will be your only visit, is that correct?"

"Oh yes." Adam beamed. "You mentioned—"

"Why such a quick departure, if I may ask?" interrupted Mr. Maatz.

Adam continued, " Well . . . I was on my way home from work two weeks ago, today, about four o'clock, I guess. And I'm just moving into the left turn lane at Twenty-eighth and Eastern when, out of the blue, I received three words from the Lord, and three times over. I never had God speak to me like that in my life! And it was as clear as if someone was sitting in the back seat of my car telling me the same thing. The words were: go back now, go back now, go back now. Just like that. And that meant go back home. Go back to Iowa."

Mr. Maatz looked stunned. "Adam! What does that indicate? Think about it! Things like that don't happen to most people. So what did you do? How did you react to this—God reaching out to YOU, Adam! And why? Why, Adam?"

A faint smile appeared. "Well, I think—or there could be two different reasons—or maybe a combination. Other than the fact that Ben got engaged and I had to move, and I went through a broken engagement and had to renege on a house deal where I had put down earnest money, I had thoughts of maybe starting something . . . asking Donny on a date. And, yeah, kind of weird to think of doing something like this after knowing him for almost twenty years, but, as I said, this was only a thought, which remained so because deep down I knew it was because of my circumstances . . . being alone . . . being without someone special. Then, too, I had thoughts of trying to find Lacie, however I could do that, which would be dangerous and stupid, so, I guess God saw everything and said, 'No, Adam. Go back home."

Adam shrugged his shoulders. "So, it was a neat experience . . . I mean, it was a miracle. I didn't question it. I accepted it. I think I may have been shocked, in a sense, because it was like . . . it was no big deal at the time. I was alone and driving a car. I mean, I can't pull over anywhere when I'm in the middle of a busy street. If someone had been with me I may have said something and shared that God just spoke to me but . . . I was . . . alone . . . and then it was so quick, a few seconds, and it's over. Then the traffic is moving so . . . But as time went on I appreciated it much more than when it first happened, and was thankful too."

"That is so amazing! I have never had a client tell me about receiving a message from the Lord Himself! " Mr. Maatz offered a prayer of thanksgiving, which Adam gladly accepted. After the prayer, Mr. Maatz offered Adam two Christian counselors that he could see when he returned to Iowa. Mr. Maatz again offered his hand to Adam and wished him a safe trip home and God's blessing.

7

Adam rented a U-haul trailer and had it all set up by Friday afternoon. He went to work with the trailer still hitched to his Celebrity to save time. When he got off work in the morning he could go straight home and start packing his belongings. He had no one to help him and it took much longer than he anticipated. He wanted to be finished and gone before Ben came home so he wouldn't have to make an awkward goodbye. Goodbyes were always awkward for Adam and he preferred to avoid them if possible.

It was near four o'clock when Adam threw the last of his clothes in the back seat. Seeing how all his clothes filled the back seat and how high the pile was gave him pause. "Really? I have this much clothing?" he thought.

The trailer was packed full and the trunk was full. He walked to the front of his Celebrity and gauged if the balance was evenly distributed. It seemed to be because the front of his car didn't seem to be elevated, but he sensed that he had a lot of weight and hoped it wouldn't be too much for the engine.

Adam discovered the significance of weight before he even reached the interstate. Approaching Ivanrest Avenue on Twenty-Eighth Street, the yellow light came on. Normally, with the distance ahead of him, he would slow down, brake, and stop, without any problems. Today, with his load, it was a different story. All he heard was a clicking sound and no slowing down whatsoever. Instinctively and immediately, he sped up, because the quicker he could enter the intersection the better it would be. The light turned red when he was twenty-five feet from entering the intersection and not one car waiting at the opposing signal started moving forward. Not even a honking horn! Once he was through, he glanced in his rearview and side mirrors and not one vehicle had started through yet. Adam couldn't help but remember and reflect on those three words. God would make sure Adam made it safely home!

But he now knew that with all the weight, he had to be very careful and wise in his driving, and he hoped by the time he approached Chicago, the traffic would not be too heavy. He certainly would not be traveling in the passing lane.

He entered Iowa just past midnight and found an easy off and on exit and a motel with few cars, which gave him all the parking and maneuverability space he needed. He was tired. It was a long day, and a lot of work. And it was hard work for his Celebrity, too. He could feel the heat of the engine or the transmission through the center console. Only another seven hours or so and he would be home.

Adam arrived home, at his mother's place, around eight o'clock the next evening. He parked on the side street and had his mother call an uncle to ask if he could come over and back Adam's car and trailer up in the driveway. He only lived a few blocks away. He didn't want to embarrass himself, or his mother, by making attempt after attempt in backing up just a two-wheeled trailer! He had done that in Michigan! His uncle was happy to come over to do the job and to see Adam. This was one of Adam's favorite uncles.

The following day he would be unloading again, but the job would not be as strenuous with a sister and brother helping out. Hopefully they would be able to help when all his belongings would have to be loaded again when he found a place to live near his new job site. He didn't want to live with his mother, not at forty-eight years of age! And he did not want to be forty-five miles from work, especially during the winter months. So the remaining days of the week would be spent finding an apartment.

Much to Adam's surprise, he found that there was very little to rent. His mother and sister scanned a local shopper paper and saw a familiar name that was related on the mother's side. He was a realtor and they decide to call him. He had no rentals but did have two houses for sale. Both houses were on the same street. He gave them the addresses and they met.

Before he showed the property, the realtor and Adam's mother engaged in conversation regarding their family history and how they were related. Adam figured that his mother's side of this family was part of the family tree but on a distant branch. But as well as they got along, as much fun as they were having, it was more like they were long lost friends.

The one house that Adam decided to look at was a small house on a lot and a half. It had a full basement and looked to be a sturdy, well-built house. The price was only eight thousand dollars in cash. Right away, Adam was interested. He inspected the interior and saw that it would need some work. Panelling in small rooms? No way. The attic was dusty and dirty but seemed to contain some relics. He hired painters to remove the panelling, and twelve layers of wallpaper, and paint the living room and restroom. It wasn't that he was afraid of work, but he hated dust and he even supplied face masks for a college couple to clean his attic.

The following year, he painted the outside of the house. He also did a bit of landscaping. He hired a fellow worker who owned a garden tiller and had him till up a narrow stretch of his yard that bordered the neighbor's yard where he wanted to plant a variety of flowers and plants, to pretty things up a bit. However, the ground was so hard that what did come up was small and weak. What did attract some attention was that on either side of the front entrance he placed half whiskey barrels, tipped over with an outpouring of colorful impatiens.

So, Adam settled in quite easily in his small home and even took in two smaller kittens from the worker who had the garden tiller. His job was going smoothly, and again it was a job at night. Adam had not had a normal daytime job for years. This job was considered a full-time job, but in reality was a part-time job. His position, as all positions on his cleaning crew, were on an incentive plan. You worked five to five and a half hours, but got paid for eight. If your equipment passed inspection, then you got your eight hours pay. If not, if production had to reclean any part of your equipment, you only got paid for hours worked. It was not very often that anyone ever had their pay docked. Thus, Adam would arrive home from work around five thirty every morning, which gave him the opportunity to seek part-time employment.

The first part-time job Adam had was delivering baked goods to grocery stores. That ended abruptly one winter morning when the van assigned to him would not warm up. There wasn't even enough heat to clear the windshield, and the van had run for an hour. He had warned the owners on the lack of heat in this van, and they had apparently decided to ignore him. So he took the keys out of the van and simply said, "It's all yours," and went home.

Next, he delivered shopper papers to towns in the area, dropping them off at homes where the kids would deliver them later in the day. This job he lost because the manager didn't realize that he would return after a short vacation. He only discovered this when another gentleman arrived and was loading his papers.

"What are you doing back?" the guy wanted to know. "You quit, they said."

Adam tried to reason with management but the decision was made .

It was about this time when Adam grew weary of his small house. From time to time he would check listings of other house and the prices just to keep informed. One day, he decided to take a different road home. He came to a stop sign on the south side of town. He turned to the north, where his small house was located, and seconds later saw a realtor's sign. The sign was in front of a story-and-a-half house on a corner lot. The large two-stall garage might have been larger than his small house! He went around the block and stopped along the side of the street to write down the realtor's number. The following day an appointment was made to see the property.

He liked what he saw. He estimated the price would be in the $50,000 to $55,000 range. To his surprise, the asking price was just below that and he made an offer of $45,000, which was accepted! But now he had to find a buyer for his small house, which he had always feared could pose a problem.

One night at work, during that same week, something happened. Usually at break time, Adam would sit at a table next to or nearest the coffee machine. Often times, he would have to make a pot of fresh coffee. This particular night, Adam was drawn to a table far from the coffee machine and sat down. Soon, two others joined him at the table. One he knew from work and he had seen him around town. They were busy talking and suddenly Adam heard, "I am looking for a house."

Immediately Adam told him that he had a house and the fact that it sits on a lot and a half is even more of a selling point. This guy wanted a place where he could put up a garage to accommodate all the cars he worked on. A lot and a half plus an alley in back was even better! He agreed to purchase Adams property for $24,000! And all this takes place within a matter of days. Within five years, he had tripled his initial investment.

The banker who handled the transactions made this comment to Adam: "I think you made a couple of really good deals here." Of course Adam had to agree! He was very happy and proud to own this house. It was almost nicer than he thought he would ever be able to own. He couldn't wait to show his family, and they in turn were surprised that he would buy a different house, and were anxious to see it. "Why do you need a bigger house?" they asked. Once all his belongings and new furniture were moved in, he had a housewarming. His mother even brought his favorite uncle along. She was so proud! Now, if he could just find an appreciative lady friend!

It wasn't long after moving into his new home that Adam found another delivery job, this one delivering office supplies. He found trouble here too. The owners hated smoke, and he was a smoker. He would smoke in the company van, but with the windows open. He even purchased air fresheners. But his efforts to alleviate the smoke smell was not sufficient and the complaints continued.

Come Valentine's Day, Adam knew a few places that seemingly had single women who would sign for his deliveries. Because he wasn't glib and didn't feel confident to start a friendly conversation, he decided to give out a few Valentine cards as an introduction, stating that he was fairly new in the area, worked weird hours, and was trying to meet new people.

Unfortunately, one woman became very upset and afraid; she called the police department and his place of employment. Her boyfriend wanted to know how Adam knew where she lived and how long he had been tailing her. Adam laughed and tried to explain that he did not know where she lived and had not been following her. He explained his intentions and that he was sorry for the confusion but that did not seem to alleviate the paranoia. Finally, Adam told the angry guy that he had his address and that he would put the front porch light on for him. Adam related this event to the manager and the following morning one of the owners called and told him that he was fired. Adam let out a laugh and said, "Fine." "Sensitivity and paranoia all the way around," he thought.

The last part-time job Adam has was driving a Head Start bus. He had this job for many years and thought that he could keep this job for as long as he wanted. Then the state money ran out and he no longer had a job. He saw a local school bus picking up kids in his town. In later shopper ads, he read that this company was still looking for more drivers, but no one contacted him. He inquired, and still nothing. Obviously, they were not interested in him driving.

Is it his age? Or could it be that he had a minor accident some years earlier? Every Saturday he would stop at a retirement home and pick up residents who wanted or needed to do a bit of shopping. The entrance of this retirement center had a curved canopy, which was too low for the bus to go under, so Adam would stop just before the entrance. One Saturday, Adam was eager to get going, not to drive the bus, but to get to his hangout in another city to possibly meet up with other men. When the number of resident shoppers were on board, Adam hurriedly got in the seat of the bus and went forward. "Bang!" He came to a sudden stop! "Oh no!" Adam cried out. He immediately knew what he had done and the reason why. He checked for bus damage and determined that he could continue with the slight damage to the top of the bus, but the real damage was to the front of the building. Many bricks, mortar, etc. had been displaced and were in need of repair. But, there was a person in need of repair too.

Then the questions began. "Why don't I see your bus anymore?" "Aren't you driving the bus anymore?" Always the questions, but from friendly, caring folks, and Adam would explain the circumstances.

So Adam now had a lot of free time. Several times during the week, he would go to a local Hardee's after the breakfast crowd was gone. There were less people around, much to his liking, and a much better chance of finding a newspaper to read and a crossword puzzle to work, if it was still blank.

One morning as he was sitting down in what he thought was the most isolated seat available, he heard a greeting. "Morning, Adam!" He gave a quick look and a quick wave of his hand and a weak "Morning," but at the time had no idea who this couple was. He was quick to get the newspaper in front of him. No other words were exchanged. He did wonder who this couple was and how they would know him. As he left, on his way to his vehicle he realized who this couple was. They were his neighbors who lived just two houses east of him, and for almost twenty years!

But that was Adam; to engage in a conversation with someone new was a real problem. He was friendly with a few of his neighbors, all single women. Two were elderly and the other were near his age but over six feet tall. They were friendly and would say "Hi," and he felt more at ease with older people. One of the older women had a rhubarb patch, which happened to be next to the taller woman's property, who also had rhubarb. Every year he had access to their rhubarb.

He was also friendly with the plumber, a home builder, repairman, and a mechanic who worked on and serviced his vehicles over the years. This was about the extent of Adam's "friends" who he was completely comfortable with in the small town where he lived.

He had friends at work and he felt sure that he was well-liked and even respected. Adam was never one to shy away from work. Several of his coworkers would kid around with him so he knew that he was well-liked. But if they only knew the real Adam!

When Adam turned fifty years of age, reality set in. He had to accept the fact that he very likely would not find a nice Christian lady to marry and have what he always had hoped for: to be a loving and nurturing Christian husband and father. And on this day, Adam became very angry at God. He laughed at God. What a joke, he thought. God smiles on some and on others He won't, regardless of their good intentions. What a waste of time.

At the same time, his brother was planning a special birthday party for him. That involved a limo that would pick up the family, drive around the city for a time, and then drop them off at a downtown hotel for an evening meal. Adam hoped he could show his appreciation and show that he indeed was having a wonderful time. Once he was home and alone he could be angry again, and he remained angry for several years. He gave away Bibles and religious tapes. "Don't need these anymore," he thought. "What's the use!"

But the accumulative effect of anger most often harbors a consequence. In Adam's case this was true. On his last break at work one night, Adam had what he thought was a brief case of heartburn. However, after work and after being home for an hour or more, he began to feel anxious. It got to the point where he could not sit still. He didn't know what to do, and he couldn't stand it, so he jumped in his vehicle and rushed to the hospital. It's around seven thirty in the morning when he was told that he was having a heart attack.

"What?" Adam cried in disbelief. "I didn't have any pain."

"Don't need to experience pain," he was told, and he was placed in an ambulance which took him to emergency in a hospital that specialized in heart care. The following morning he received an angioplasty, and two days later was home. He had no recurrent health problems, except he did have a carotid artery in his neck cleaned, or scraped, some years later. Subsequent physicals indicated that his heart was not damaged in any way from the heart attack.

And after many years, the anger slowly disappeared and Adam again found forgiveness and love for God; yet, his inability to overcome his past still haunted him. Why couldn't he be a more responsible Christian? Why couldn't he feel comfortable in a church with God's people but could feel comfortable with people who were abominable like he was? And how many times did he hope that he left his home quietly enough early on a Sunday morning so his neighbors wouldn't notice, and travel fifteen miles to the next town and have an Egg McMuffin and an order of hotcakes, while leisurely going through the Sunday paper. And depending on the time, get home before his neighbors, or get home as everyone else was coming home from church. But after playing this game for so many years, including the times in Michigan, there came a time where he didn't care anymore.

He did hear a broadcast one Sunday and determined that he would attend a service at this church because he enjoyed the sermon and the minister, Unfortunately, most of the songs this church would sing were new-age praise songs that Adam didn't know. He loved to sing, but he loved to sing the old favorite hymns that no one ever tired of singing. This church would sing a familiar hymn once in awhile, but the last time he attended this church, not one song did he know, and he never returned.

Adam visited other churches, and to his dismay discovered the same thing. What he did notice was that when an old hymn was sung the decibel level rose significantly. So, the congregation would praise the Lord more in singing an old favorite hymn than a new-age song. Another thing he noticed was not one of these new-age songs that he had heard, and tried to sing, could compare in melody or in message. Was he the only one who noticed this? Didn't worship leaders notice? Ministers either? Frustrated, Adam ceased visiting churches. He always felt out of place anyway, felt like he couldn't fit in, so why fight it any longer?

Soon, he began to think of retiring. Because of the national debt, he had to work nine months beyond his sixty-fifth birthday before he could retire. Little did he know that he would eventually work well beyond his retirement age. He reasoned that he was only working part-time anyway, and what would he do every day? Plus, he liked the guys he was working with, and liked the job, except for the inspections, which would drive everyone crazy. But, once home and away from that environment, a new day would emerge, a different time, and another go-round.

When Adam did retire, it wasn't long before he realized that he no longer wanted the responsibility of owning his home—of mowing the lawn or shoveling snow or the general upkeep of maintaining a nice home. Of course, he really didn't have a home. He only had a house.

Over the years, from time to time Adam would think about his life and why things happened as they did. After more serious thought, he decided that maybe God wanted him to write his life story. He found a few attractive diary books, he assumed, with lines on the pages. "Just what he needed," he thought. He started writing one week and amassed perhaps twenty-five pages! Some accomplishment!

But when he went to review it, he discovered that 50 percent of what he had written was illegible! He did make another attempt, but the lines were closer together and after only a few pages of trying to write as carefully and legibly as he could, he gave up on the idea, and his desire to write his story was shelved. There were other things to concentrate on.

Thus, he began to clear out a junk room, which he so often would look into and quickly close the door because he couldn't decide where to start. He decided to start by throwing out things he no longer needed, things that he no longer was interested in, and old magazines and books that smelled of dewy mold. For several weeks, his city trash barrel was overflowing and on either side was a box or two of those books and magazines.

He also made several trips to Goodwill and to a mission store. He then cleaned out his garage and began to bring in items for a garage sale. Almost every weekend he would have a garage sale. He also was told that he should try Craigslist and a cousin suggested Facebook with all their swap shops. But first he needed a class to become a bit familiar with a computer. After some time, and with assistance from the library staff, he was able to post photos of much of what he had for sale.

It took much longer to sell his things than what he thought. He even had to close down one winter, and begin again when the weather warmed up. In the end, he donated what remaining furniture he had and boxed the remaining valuables that he was not going to give away.

Mowing his grass one day, for the last time he hoped, he began to feel pain in his legs. Usually, the time spent mowing his lawn was no more than twenty-five minutes. He could only finish the lawn in front of the house. He could barely make it to the garage to put the mower away. Later in the week he has a doctor's appointment. He had a difficult time getting ready for it, He was that weak. He drove himself to the clinic, found a wheelchair that was available in the entrance, and simply waited for someone to be of assistance. Upon seeing a doctor he was told that he had pneumonia and was hospitalized. Three days later he was back home and had just enough strength to sweep out the garage before the sale of his house was finalized. Lacking the strength and energy for a major move, he hired a mover, and within two days was almost entirely settled into his one-bedroom apartment.

In the process of gaining experience on a computer and seeing the word "save," a thought occurred to him. Would it be possible to write his story on a computer and save it? He asked a staff member of the library if that was possible. Of course it was, and soon Adam was at the library almost every day doing something he never thought he would do.

8

Two years later on a Monday morning in February, Adam awakened and did not have the energy or the desire to arise, even to make a fresh pot of coffee or to make a light breakfast. He immediately realized what this feeling was. It was depression, and was determined that he would not let this be a part of his life. He knew that somewhere on his desk he had a phone number for counseling that he had torn off a notice he spotted on the bulletin board at a grocery store. He had torn it off just in case. Well, he had a case for it now, but he would search for it when he got up—whenever that might be.

It wasn't until noon that he finally arose. He made a pot of coffee and had a bowl of cereal and a slice of toast with dandelion jam. He then found the phone number and made an appointment, which was set for the following Wednesday. Thankful and satisfied, he returned to the couch where he laid for most of the day.

He entered the center for counseling and right away liked the ambiance. He liked the art prints on the walls, the reception and seating areas looked comforting, and the receptionist was very friendly with a nice smile.

"Are you Adam?"

He moved away from the seating area to the reception counter. "Yes, that's me."

The receptionist had papers for him to fill out. "Just a few questions we'd like you to answer so we can know you better, OK?"

"OK," Adam agreed and returned to the seating area.

Finishing the questions, Adam took the forms to the counter where a gentleman in slacks and a print shirt was waiting. "I'm Mark. Welcome to our facility. We have coffee, tea, or some sodas, whatever is left. I'll meet you just around the corner to your left, OK?""

Adam followed the directions and saw what could be described as a mini kitchen.

"So what'll it be, Adam, coffee or tea, or—"

"Coffee is fine. Straight, no sugar or cream."

"Got it," was the answer he heard. "Find a seat in the room across the hall there and I'll be there in just a sec," Mark instructed Adam as he pointed to the room.

It was a small but comfortable room, with a small round table and a lamp and two chairs on either side. There was also a bookshelf with books and a desk area with a computer. Mark entered the room with two cups and set them on a magazine. He opened a drawer at the desk area and found two coasters that he placed on the table. He then placed the two cups of coffee on the coasters.

After some chitchat, Mark directed his attention to the forms that Adam had filled out previously.

"I see that you list depression as your problem today. Has that been an ongoing issue?"

Adam took a sip of his coffee. "Well, I think from what I've learned over the years that I've probably had clinical depression to varying degrees, but just lived with it . . . just put up with it. But what I experienced Monday was not the same. That was something different. That had me down. I did not want to get up . . . to do anything . . . period. I never felt like that before."

Mark was sitting forward resting his arms on his knees. "I must commend you for acting as quickly as you did."

Adam took another sip of coffee. "Well, I knew right away that this was not something I was going to let stand. I was not going to live with this every day. No way!"

Mark again looked at the forms Adam had completed. "I see here that you are divorced. Would that have anything to do with your depression? Any ongoing disagreements, child-rearing—"

"No, no," Adam interrupted. "That happened long ago. We have no communication. Actually, the marriage never should have happened."

Mark looked puzzled. "Would you like to explain the circumstances for me?"

Adam looked away, shaking his head. "I was not well . . . emotionally . . . psychologically . . . whatever. I mean . . . part of my problem, or problems, is that I'm a product of my past. I was covertly rejected, neglected, had no sexual identity, as I was told by a counselor, and only a few years ago discovered that what I have experienced over the years had a name for it: social anxiety disorder. And years earlier, I was watching one of those afternoon talk shows on TV and this one show scrolled twelve different symptoms on the screen which I could relate to . . . totally . . . except two I think. Anyway, these symptoms were the results of childhood sexual abuse. So, I have a past—you have no idea. But as for the marriage, I went through a period in dating this girl, underage at the time, where I was impulsive and completely irresponsible. Why, I have no idea. I have no explanation, I really don't. And eventually, she got pregnant."

"And this was how long ago?" Mark wanted to know.

"Oh," Adam sighed. "Back in sixty-six, sixty-seven maybe."

"Ah," Mark sat back in his chair. "Back then, you get a girl pregnant, you get married."

"Yeah," Adam nodded. "And just before the wedding, I had all my bags packed, sitting in the living room. I was sitting on the couch ready to leave, but I wasn't sure where to go. Then too, I couldn't disappear and put my family in turmoil, especially my mother. So, yeah . . . not a pleasant experience at all—a living nightmare."

"So, I'm curious," offered Mark. "What happened? How long did the marriage last?"

"Legally, a little over a year. But, before that, I can remember coming home from work one day, and here sitting on our couch with my wife is my mother. She just knew something was wrong. And this isn't that long after the marriage . . . like six weeks or so, and I don't remember who really makes an appointment with a psychiatrist in Cherokee but I begin seeing him on a weekly basis. And I don't think these weekly meetings last that long. I do remember that he wanted me to draw a picture of a man and a woman. I wasn't good at drawing so I drew stick figures. I also remember looking at those inkblot cards.

"Some weeks later, I'm at a bar drinking, feeling sorry for myself, and have thoughts of taking a blade and slashing my wrists. And you know . . . I don't think I was really that serious about it . . . but, I go to a pay telephone booth inside this bar and call this psychiatrist's number. His wife answers and I tell her my thoughts. She says that he is in a meeting and to hold on while she tries to get in touch with him. I'm waiting and waiting, and all of a sudden there's two, three, maybe four police officers, lifting me from that phone booth and dragging me out, through the bar, to the police car, and I'm crying like a baby! I spend the night in a cell, and don't remember what happened the following day. No one knows that this happened, even my wife. I had moved out, so she had no idea.

"I'm not even sure if my employer knew what happened. But, the following day I was back to work servicing vending machines. And apparently I was doing a really good job. The increase in sales was substantial, to the point that my route was taking in the most money. I then was promoted to sandwich, soup, and beverage machines."

"You must have been a good worker," Mark added.

Adam agreed with a nod. "I always was a good worker . . . thank God What was beneficial for me, I think, in most of the jobs I had, was that I was in part the only one responsible for the job I had to do. But to start a new job . . . a new position and have people watch you, was nerve-racking for me. I hated that. But after I became comfortable on the job, I was fine."

Mark sat up in his chair and folded his arms across his chest. "Sounds like you could do quite well outside the home, on the job, but couldn't do the job at home."

Adam agreed. "That's one way to put it. I was in a lot of turmoil, confusion, and just didn't know how to deal with it—didn't want to deal with it. I mean, when I was eighteen years old, I knew something had not gone right growing up. And already, at that age, I sensed it had to do with my father. So, my hope was that one day I would be a loving, nurturing, Christian husband and father with a wonderful family. And look what I end up with!

"Difficult to accept," Mark said. "So, eventually what happens? How do things work out and what about the child?"

"Well," Adam nodded as he began, "I kind of come to my senses in the end. We have been separated for awhile, and I realize that what I've always wanted, I have. That's a wife and a little girl, both who need a loving, nurturing husband and father, and I think that maybe I should take responsibility and try and make this work. So, the weekend is coming and my plan is to stop by the apartment on a friday evening and tell her I want to take her out to eat. I then, at some point, will tell her that I want to try and work this out. But, I get to the apartment, and she isn't home. A neighbor says that she is out with a shoe salesman. I don't see her all that weekend, and my plan falls by the wayside, but I still have some hope things may work out.

"We do reconnect as friends and I stop in to visit her and my daughter. Then one day in September of sixty-nine I stop in, and she says, 'Guess what?' She tells me that our divorce has been finalized, much to my surprise. And I'm shocked. I say something to the effect that I might as well leave and walk out the door. She breaks down and cries, saying, 'But I still love you!' It is then that I decide to return to Michigan, and I leave over Memorial Day weekend. We keep in touch and I, along with my sister, make it back to Iowa, usually twice a year, once during the summer and at Christmas time."

Mark still had questions. "So you would see her and your daughter twice a year?"

"Usually, yes," Adam said. "In fact, the following year I spent a day and a half with them."

"So, was there any bonding between you and your daughter?" Mark asked.

Adam let out a sigh. "Unfortunately, not. I only saw her twice a year, always with her mother present. I would send her birthday cards, Christmas cards, Valentine's Day cards, but never received any cards from her. Then, too, she never had my name, Her mother gave her her maiden name, so that always upset me. Then, as a teenager I would hear from her personally, but that was usually because she needed or wanted money for something. She even accused me one time of not caring about her . . . which didn't sit very well with me either. And, after that . . . I . . . just kind of forgot about her, forgot about being a proper father figure. I mean, sad to say, I really didn't care. It's that cold, dark, space within me that I've always felt."

Mark sat up in his chair, his interest heightened. "That sounds intriguing. What can you tell me about that?"

Adam then offered to tell Mark his life story. "If you need a refill on coffee, better get it, 'cause it isn't a short story, OK?"

Mark was surprised. "Oh . . . OK. Let me check the front desk just a sec and I'll be right back."

Adam went through the gruelling task of retelling his story once again to a counselor. After he finished, he sat back, and made a simple request. "Now, I would like a refill!"

Mark jumped up from his chair. "Absolutely! Be right back!" He returned with Adam's refill and offered him his assessment. "That is quite the story you have, Adam. And those three words, three times over . . . what a WOW moment! Words unspoken yet still heard, right?"

"Yes. Absolutely. Thank God," Adam replied after a sip of his coffee.

Mark continued. "I have two things I want to suggest to you. First, I have three words for you too: serious emotional abandonment. Does that make sense to you?

Adam sat his cup on a coaster. "Man . . . that makes more sense than anything else I've heard over the years. That definitely makes sense."

"Secondly," Mark continued, "You didn't mention this, but in my estimation, you became, and were, a bisexual addict—all your adult life. That could be difficult to admit but—"

"No, no." Adam broke in. "You are right, and it isn't hard for me to admit it. When a guy runs to an adult theatre in the morning and then picks up a girl on the street that evening, that's being an addict . . . not that this is what I did on a daily basis, but it did happen. And even when I was in relationships, I still did these things, so . . . yeah." Adam looked at Mark and nodded.

"OK. Secondly," Mark began as he looked at his notes, "We— you—will never know for sure what happened to you as a child un- less you suddenly have a memory of it, but I do think something happened to you, and it wouldn't surprise me at all if whatever that was, it took away or affected your innocence. Why do I say that? I'm just connecting the dots, so to speak. You said that what was so spe- cial with Lacie was that it was all in innocence; that she was naïve and innocent and that is what attracted you. And, that you felt so comfortable with her, and even with your neighbor girl, you said the same thing. So, I'm wondering if that inner child didn't have that in- nocence taken from you, and that is why you are attracted to young girls. It's a possibility is all I'm saying, OK? And, there are those symp- toms that you saw on TV that you could relate to, so . . .

"Another thing: you mentioned that you thought that you must have been a lonely child, but you have no memory of feeling lonely. Now, you were basically alone without playmates in your age bracket for some time. At six, seven, and eight years of age, who was there on the farm who could play with you? This, too, could be the reason that you are attracted to girls of this age."

Adam smiled and nodded in agreement. "That makes sense too. But, from what I know or understand about this . . . stuff, is that if I were sexually abused, I think I would have shown some serious symptoms, like acting out—especially at the time I began exposing myself, you know?"

Mark looked up in thought. "You have a point—a valid point . All of this is merely what is, or could be, possible . . . except for the emotional abandonment."

Adam said nothing, but just nodded in agreement.

Mark rose from his chair. "You OK? I don't want to cause you any more confusion or give you more things to mull over in your mind without any firm conclusions."

"No, not at all—nothing like that. It's just that I've been presented with so much to think about . . . which I did not expect, so . . . thank you." Adam also rose from his chair. "I even feel better . . . just talking with someone, I guess. Just wish I had done this years ago."

Mark then had an idea. "Well, on that note, how would you like a mentor? Would you like someone to talk to, to go out for coffee with once a week?"

Adam smiled and a slight frown appeared. "A mentor? I could have used a mentor fifty years ago. Little late for a mentor now, I would think, but having a friend to have coffee with on occasion would be a welcome change, being as I have no friend to have coffee with. Well, let me be more specific: I have no male friend to have coffee with. I do have a female friend that I've had coffee dates with. So . . . sure. They say that you can never have too many friends."

"OK. Good. I'll give your name to our mentor coordinator and she can get in touch with you a bit later." Mark shook Adam's hand, put his left hand on Adam's shoulder, and said, "Thanks for sharing your story, and God's blessing to you my friend. Is it OK with you if we put you on our prayer list?"

Adam was quick to say, "Yes! Yes! I would appreciate that. Thank you!" As he left the center, he wondered, was it God who urged him to tear off that slip of paper with the center's number on it? Whatever, he was pleased with how well things went and looked forward to meeting a new friend.

9

The following week Adam met his mentor at the center. He was a choir leader, a part-time worship leader, a Christian gentleman, and a Christian jack of all trades. If he had some free time and if anyone needed any kind of assistance, he was available. They met with the coordinator and discussed issues, interests, and times they want to meet, and set up a schedule . They decided to meet for coffee every Thursday afternoon at two o'clock. Once the details were agreed to, it was suggested that Adam and his mentor, Tim, spend some time together and become acquainted.

Once again, Adam told his story. Later, as they conversed, Adam sensed that Tim had a little interest or knowledge in emotional or psychological issues, which would aid in understanding him.

He did ask Adam about his marriage. "You haven't seen your daughter for how many years now?"

Adam had to think. "Well, that's a good question. The last time I saw her was when she was a teenager . . . maybe thirteen, fourteen years old. She is late forties now, so . . . it's been a while. So, I would say that we are estranged . . . unfortunately. And, I think it's safe to say that we all had a part in that, including my ex, but, you know . . . human nature, as it can be . . . especially with flawed people." Adam shrugged. "What can one expect in difficult situations? I'm not happy about it, yet it's been going on for so long that after a while, it's just not a big deal anymore. You become hardened to it."

"I guess I can understand that," Tim added. "So how long have

THREE WORDS FOR A VULNERABLE MAN

you been retired and what do you do to keep yourself busy?"

"Just for a couple of years," Adam replied. "Before moving, I spent a lot of time on a computer at the library trying to sell my belongings and having garage sales on weekends. After that I began writing my life story."

Tim was surprised. "Really? So how is that going?"

Adam looked away. "Yeah . . . I'm not sure. I mean, this is something that I've never done before. I have no idea what is involved in publishing, or how much it will cost. So far I've got around fifteen thousand words and they want at least sixteen thousand, preferably twenty-thousand words, so . . . and then there's no one around to get any advice from either. Right now all I'm focusing on is getting the words down, so I can read them," Adam laughed as he recalled his previous attempts in writing and discovering that he couldn't read his own handwriting. "So it's a work in progress."

Tim and Adam met every week for approximately a year. Their mentor advisor unexpectedly retired to focus on a growing family. For the summer of their second year they decide to take a break for three months and resume their meetings in September.

In the meantime, Adam continued his visits to the library and worked on his story. He decided to start over to see if he could produce more words. After much thought and several letters that he threw away, he finally wrote a letter that he kept to send to Lacie. But first, he needed to find her address and logs onto The Yellow Pages. He discovered that she had a different address from the last letter he sent, to which he did not receive a reply.

He sent the letter during the week and estimated that the letter should arrive that weekend. Monday morning he made his way as usual to the library. Near the end of checking his emails, he found one from Michigan, from a police department! Apparently, Lacie was not happy about receiving his letter and any further contact would produce an arrest warrant! What an interesting story that would be! Imagine the headline: "Man Arrested For Writing Letter." Then, news reporters would want to know what was in the letter, and then they would question the arresting officers, "Why was this gentleman was arrested!"

In the letter, Adam only informed Lacie that he was writing his life story, which at some point, involved her. He asked her if she would be kind enough to express her thoughts and feelings from that time, and what transpired after he left; he would be happy to send her fifty dollars per sheet of paper. He even offered her any possible royalties, and said that if anyone in ensuing years became familiar with "their story" and thought it could make an interesting movie, she could have full control. After all, by then he would more than likely be gone! But as it was now apparent, she had absolutely no interest. He wondered if she even read the letter. This was the third time that Adam had reached out to her and every time it was not a positive outcome. So many times Adam had wondered why. And now, after almost thirty years, why would she still have so much anger and hate? For Adam, it appeared that this would be an unsolved mystery that he would take to his grave, along with his unrequited love. If only he had listened to that feeling of not becoming involved—and yet, his story would not be nearly as interesting!

Adam did receive a surprise "friend" request on Facebook that thrilled him; it was from his daughter! After the last angry letter that he had received from her, he figured that this would indeed spell the very end of an already long-lasting estrangement. As a Vietnam veteran, he had even wondered who he could designate to receive the flag at his funeral.

The request was friendly, and apparently when she saw his photo on his Facebook page, she thought that he looked really sick and perhaps was near death! Consequently, she thought that she should contact him. Just another act of God, watching over him, Adam thought. And for the first time in his life, he actually felt love for his daughter and wanted to see her. So there was hope for a positive ending for a family that never was a real family.

What a difference a day makes!

EPILOGUE

I mentioned how I became acquainted with a computer and knowing enough to post photos of items I wanted to sell before selling my house. From time to time, because of my interest in news and politics, I would click on various Craigslist political posts just to see what others were saying. One day, an image of Martin Luther King Jr. appeared on the screen with these words, "Nothing in all the world is more dangerous than sincere ignorance and conscientious stupidity."

I've always found quotes fun to read. They tend to be words of wisdom, or quite humorous. This quote stunned me with it's content. I immediately thought of liberals, but soon dismissed that because my attention went to two words: "sincere" and "conscientious." Why, I didn't know. Why were these words used? What was their purpose? How could they be described? I even asked the staff at my library about these words and received no answer. I knew, other than being a part of sentence parsing, they were modifiers, but there was something else I needed, or wanted, to know. For several days I could not find an answer, so I gave it a rest.

When I returned to attempt to solve my word problem, I simply put the quote in front of me and stared at it, studied it. It wasn't long before I realized that the quote was a single entity, but it contained two conditions: ignorance and stupidity. Thus, those troublesome words, other than being modifiers, were also words that defined these unfortunate conditions and gave life and legitimacy to ignorance and stupidity. They were, and are, real.

Finally, I had solved this problem and was a bit proud of myself. "A job nicely done," I thought as I began to rise from the computer table, only to be pulled back by another word: "dangerous."

Dangerous? "Nothing is more dangerous than" . . . what? It wasn't war, earthquakes, storms, fires, or floods. No, it wasn't anything physical. What was it then? It didn't take long before I realized that the most " dangerous" thing is fallen man, or myself! And a huge spotlight suddenly began to shine on me and my life.

In the process of writing and remembering things, and as I approached the ending of my story, I realized that all through my emotionally sin-scarred life, God was always there watching over me, keeping me safe from certain danger, maybe even death. He was, as we read in scripture, "The Good Shepherd." And to bring more emphasis and significance to how God acted in my life, I thought I would chronicle it in these final words.

My very first experience of God came when I was approximately three to three and a half years of age. I was with my parents, who attended a showing of a Billy Graham Crusade on a large screen at our local high school auditorium. This had to be sometime in 1944. When the invitation was given for those who wanted to come forward to receive Christ, I immediately wanted to go forward. I looked up to my mother, but she was looking off to the right where the invitation was offered. I can still see her standing there, her hands resting on the folding chair in front of her, and it appeared that she was wearing a knit sweater. But, I said nothing, and who knows why? And how is a child to respond to something like this, out of the blue? I believe that God allowed that incident to tell me today, that this was the time He chose me to make His choice real to me. Not saying anything to my mother reminds me of the time when I was in my own upstairs bedroom for the first time and things were moving and it frightened me. I called for Mother but I didn't express any fear of these things moving in my room. No, I just wanted a drink of water! Two nights in a row I did this. After the second night, apparently things stopped moving!

And remember me and that little red wagon? Did God prevent

me from falling in a way that I hit my eyebrow rather than that lever penetrating my eye?

I mentioned the close call when Walt and I first left Iowa for Michigan. This may have been God's first intervention in saving me from harm or death. More incidents would occur.

Shortly after arriving in Michigan, I had a sense that something had not been right in my childhood. I wondered, too, if God really loved me or cared about me. So I prayed and asked God to show me that he cared for me. That very week, on three occasions, I had cars run a red light and whiz by so quickly in front of me that I didn't even have time to put on my brakes! After the third time, I realized that this was how God was answering my prayer. And, in my estimation, this is the most significant answer of prayer that I have received in my life, or that I am consciously aware of. That had never occured before, and hasn't since.

At some point as a teenager, the joy of singing hymns became apparent. It just made my heart feel so blessed. Since that time, I continue to enjoy singing and listening to choirs.

It was much later in my life when I heard the song "The Unclouded Day," and I burst into tears. This was a song about heaven, where no storm clouds would roll.

I had a similar experience one day reading Ephesians 1:4, which, other than John 3:16, is one of the most significant and awesome verses in the Bible. I'm sure that I had read this verse previously, but on this particular day the Holy Spirit, again, decided to touch the spirit within me and again I wept. Here's a God who, before He formed this earth, thought of me—knew me!

There was a day, too, when the first line of the Lord's Prayer became more prominent for me. I had a Father in heaven who could do much more for me than any earthly father could.

Now, even though I had these experiences, I was still living my adulterous and abominable life. In 1971, I awoke one morning and something was different. The previous night, I had prayed about a relationship that was troubled with someone that I really cared about. I awoke and was happy! Then I noticed that I felt one hundred pounds lighter! I physically felt lighter on my feet! I had experienced a re-birth. That is how it feels when God takes away your sin. I even had confidence. Fear was gone. A day or two later I was visiting friends at the noon hour and they asked me if I would ask a blessing. I did without hesitation. That would not have happened before. Unfortunately, this spiritual euphoria only lasted a few weeks and I was back to doing the same things as before, much to my disappointment.

One day in Vietnam, I was in the first wave of helicopters to land at a site where my unit hoped to set up operations. We had been in a holding pattern for several weeks. After a minute or two, we came under gunfire. I heard bullets whistling by my head, and had dirt kicked up in my face as more bullets hit the ground beside me. Why was I standing at that very spot so I didn't get hit? Incident number two?

Years later, God was still watching over me, even in Iowa. I mentioned the houses I bought and sold and how God worked all that out so quickly. I was in the second house one late summer day when I noticed that my water had an odor to it. It didn't look dirty, so I thought I would wait and see if the city knew that there was a problem, and the odor would eventually disappear. That didn't happen. So I called my plumber.

Apparently, if I remember correctly, there were some copper pipes that were going bad. He removed them and said that it would take care of the odor but he recommended that I get a new hot water heater within a year. I noticed at that time some rust at the very bottom. I decided then that I would use the following year's tax refund to buy a new water heater and forgot about it.

But, God didn't forget. One day, out of the blue, I'm guessing possibly two months before Christmas, I got the idea of calling the bank to see if I could get an early Christmas cash loan before they offered them to the public, so I could buy a water heater. They agreed to the interest-free loan. I called my plumber and we made the necessary arrangements.

On the day he was to install the new water heater, I left my house open for him as I went for a cup of coffee and to get a few grocery items. I came home and noticed a ladder on my deck off the kitchen. "Odd," I thought, as I put away my groceries.

I then heard my name called from the basement.

"Come down here a minute," the plumber said. I immediately descended the stairs. "How have you been feeling lately?" he asked me.

The only thing that I can answer is that I have had some very minor headaches, nothing more. He told me that while working on replacing my water heater he began to feel "loony." He noticed that where he was working was a chimney and he put two and two together and checked the top of my chimney outside—it was plugged with a bird's nest! I had carbon monoxide entering my basement, which would have been in greater quantity the colder it became. I rate this act of God as third most significant.

The number one act of God in my life is when he impressed those three words upon my mind, and three times over: "Go back now, go back now, go back now."

What so impressed me, and yet depressed me too, was the fact that God was totally faithful to me even while most of my adult life I lived as an abominable, bisexual addict, not to mention the time I completely gave up on Him when I turned fifty. But He was faithful, even when I wasn't.

A recent devotional talked about spiritual maturity. That word "maturity" struck a chord within me. It was almost like the final dot appeared that I could connect to and explained why I could develop strong feelings for an underage girl.

If one is emotionally abandoned, without adequate and proper sexual identification and without love that is shown or displayed, there is then no nurturing, no bonding, and nothing for a child to model after, or to identify with. In other words, there is no connection. Thus, there is no emotional or psychological maturation. And if that leaves a hole, a void in one's psyche, that "inner child" may harbor deep feelings, and in unexpected compromising situations—boys or men, or underage girls—men like myself can easily and quickly succumb. I think I was that vulnerable.

Yes, I am acquainted with homosexuality and with pedophilia, unfortunately. But if God had not been watching over me, it's very possible I could be an openly gay man and even be proud of it! Or, I could be sitting in prison as a sex offender.

In retrospect, my tale is an example in triplicate. First, it's an example of my parental neglect. Secondly, I'm an example of the results of that neglect; thirdly, I'm an example of how faithful and gracious God is to His children.

In closing, for parents I would recommend Dr. James Dobson's books on raising sons and on raising daughters. For young people, especially addicts, Neil T. Anderson has several excellent books available that I found enlightening. Enter his name on a computer and his books will pop up.

2

It has been several months now, and yet, here I am! First of all, my original choice to publish my manuscript decided not to publish, apparently due to the content. Consequently, I've been searching for another publisher, albeit, not vigorously. Secondly, I must comment on my lack of professional ability. Once I was satisfied with what I had written, I was puzzled and troubled, to a point. If my true name is on the cover of my book, why then is my name different in the story? Why did I do that? Was that acceptable? It seemed odd, and unprofessional! So for some weeks I pondered whether I should start over and change my story to present past tense or whatever tense it would be! I have no idea! See, I am not a professional! But, I really did not have the energy, or even the will to undertake such a task, again! Also, I have problems of laziness, or it is possible that it's a mild form of clinical depression, or, perhaps even ADD. Maybe it's a combination of all three! Whatever it is, this is something I think I've had to varying degrees all my adult live. And, being older and alone, it doesn't get any better. There are days that I don't get moving until one or two o'clock! So I have decided that Adam stays!

For any of you who can identify with what I have experienced, what I found that gave me comfort was a (cherry) wooden cross I purchased. It is a nice size, approximately fourteen by seven inches. It was made to hang on a wall, but I keep it on my coffee table. Sometimes when I'm feeling sad, or sorry for myself, I take that cross and place it over my heart as I fall asleep. I also, on many occasions, when I feel Satan's attacks and temptations, will take that cross and proclaim in a stern voice, in every room, "In Jesus's name, I command you, Satan, be gone! Be out of this room!" I do this in every room and when I get near the entryway I even open the door, with a final "Get out!" The first time I did this, I was surprised by how quickly I was relieved. This idea came from Mr. Andersons's book on bondage.

Have any of you at various times realized something significant, seemingly for the first time, yet when you think about it, you think that you should have known whatever it is all your life? When I was a young adult, and a Christian, I think I knew this, but I know I never gave it a thought—that is, that there is right and wrong, and good and evil. And who knows you almost as well as God? Satan! And when you are handicapped because of neglect in your childhood, "The Great Deceiver," "The Father of Lies," will win out more often than not. And you aren't even aware of it. That could very well be what Martin Luther King Jr. described as being sincerely ignorant. That is why it is so important to seek counseling and/or find a mentor. I certainly wish I had done so.

I wonder too if many of us with whatever difficulties we have don't forget who we are as believers. I would like to expand on Ephesians 1:4.

But first one must believe the Bible. Second Timothy 3:16 says that "All scripture is inspired." The key word in this verse is "all." All scripture, every verse, is inspired, not just some of it. And why it is inspired is for our benefit. One example of that benefit is for our "correction." To quote a Bible verse to supposedly make a point in an argument is just for one's convenience. This is seen most often in those who believe in gay marriage. How is God to bless an abomination? Spiritually, this does not compute. I'm reminded of a female minister who was on a talk show years ago. She was a member of a swingers club and apparently she spiritually rationalized it was OK to freely have sex with whoever! And the following Sunday, go to her church and preach a sermon! Incredible! Then too, we have to remember that God "is the same yesterday, today, and forever" (Hebrews 13:8).

He does not change with the culture. (Sorry!) Also, as I have experienced, He will "never leave you nor forsake you" (Hebrews 13:5).

Now, back to that verse in Ephesians. Not only did God know me, and you, before He formed this earth, but He "formed us in our mother's womb" (Isaiah 44:2). In other words, God gave us our psyche. God gave me my sensitivity, my intellectual capability, my work ethic, all my likes and dislikes. Or, He led me in areas that would benefit me. And I wasn't even aware of it!

And yet, there were areas I visited where He did not lead me! That is when Satan had led me, and I allowed it. When one is lacking and vulnerable in emotional issues, that need for attention, affection, or acceptance can so easily supersede one's spiritual need and/or maturity. Now, in my old age, I understand that! Too little too late? Not at all! The way I process my life is that God allowed my life to happen as it did. I am, and my life is, as I mentioned, an example for others—for parents and for victims. I hope there are at least a few who can learn from my experiences.

It is said that we are all a product of our past. I realized this some years ago. Then I realized that I allowed myself to be a product of my past. I then made a serious attempt to make a few changes. But when you're uncomfortable in public, socially inept, invariably you say or do something that is not appropriate, and you get that look! So, you remain the same product! You remain aloof, distant, and keep to yourself so you're not an embarrassment.

So that is where I'm at today, and I'm OK with that. I've been a loner all my life and I'll end my life being alone. After a while I think one becomes hardened to being alone. I really have no desire to find a partner. If that is still in my future, then God will do it! But at this point in my life I just want His daily presence and hope for more of his leading.

When you allow yourself to be a product of your past,
you can walk a lonely road.

www.ingramcontent.com/pod-product-compliance
Lightning Source LLC
LaVergne TN
LVHW091230080426
835509LV00009B/1228